THE

GREAT BRAIN

ROBBERY

Tom Scott & Trevor Grice

ALLEN&UNWIN

This edition published in 2005

First published in 1996

Allen & Unwin
83 Alexander Street
Crows Nest NSW 2065
Phone: (61 2) 8425 0100
Fax: (61 2) 9906 2218
Email: info@alleandunwin.com
Web: www.allenandunwin.com

National Library of Australia
Cataloguing-in-Publication entry:

Scott, Tom (Thomas) 1947 -
    The great brain robbery : what everyone should know about
    teenagers and drugs.

    2nd ed.

    ISBN 1 74114 640 2.

    1. Substance abuse. 2. Brain - Effect of drugs on. 3.
    Teenagers - Drug use. 4. Drugs of abuse. I. Grice, Trevor,
    1932- . II. Title.

362.29

Printed in Australia by BPA Print Group
10 9 8 7 6 5 4 3 2 1

CONTENTS

CONTENTS

Part 2 - The Danger List 67
FROM ALCOHOL TO STEROIDS: A READY-REFERENCE GUIDE TO ALL THE MAJOR DRUGS

This section provides itemised information about all the most common drugs from alcohol to heroin. This section, which is in alphabetical order, can be used as a ready-reference guide to the origins, ingredients, effects and dangers of drugs.

Part 3 - The Hard Science 110
This section explains in more detail how nerve impulses are generated, transmitted and interfered with in the brain.

"Possession
isn't nine-tenths
of the law,
it's nine-tenths
of the problem."

John Lennon

INTRODUCTION

WHY WE WROTE THIS BOOK

I am a child of the 60s. I went to Massey University at the height of Flower Power and flatted in a series of dilapidated old houses in Palmerston North in New Zealand. In one flat I painted a giant mural of Jimi Hendrix on one wall and the chemical formula of LSD in special paint on another. The formula glowed with a ghostly luminescence under the fluorescent light we were very proud of. It was at a party where "A Day in the Life" from Sgt Pepper was being played over and over that I saw my first joint being passed around.

Tom Scott

Not being a smoker I couldn't suck on burning vegetable matter without my throat hurting or my eyes watering copiously. I was having enough difficulty impressing girls as it was, so I decided it would seem hipper to refuse than to double over coughing and spluttering. I didn't indulge then, and don't now, but I defended other people's right to.

When my own children reached the age when indulging became a possibility, I began to re-examine my position. Other teenagers who smoked marijuana regularly - children of my friends and friends of my children - were dropping out of school and getting into trouble. It was then that I began to suspect that marijuana wasn't quite as benign as was commonly assumed.

This suggestion is anathema to many of my contemporaries and colleagues in the media. Cannabis (the plant from which marijuana comes) has enjoyed a good press from my generation - the ruling wisdom being that if getting stoned wasn't exactly good for you, it did you little harm either, and in the process you had a nice time and - if you were really lucky - received insights into the mysteries of the cosmos.

Historically the case against marijuana has relied more on anecdotal evidence than on hard data. The "reefer madness" foaming at the mouth, anti-marijuana propaganda films of the 40s, didn't exactly help the debate. Authoritative drug research is costly and time-consuming, and in the past the various disciplines involved have tended to work in isolation, with the result that their findings have been piecemeal and sometimes contradictory.

Some social scientists, self-appointed experts and assorted lobbyists call for more lenient attitudes to cannabis use, on the grounds that it is "less harmful than alcohol" and that marijuana is an exception to the rule that recreational drugs have toxic side effects. This mantra, echoed by an often gullible media, has drowned out the polite demurrings of research chemists, toxicologists, neuro-physiologists and clinicians.

Indeed, up until recently it was possible to defend cannabis on the grounds that the jury was still out. Not any longer. Scientists from around the world have filed back into the courtroom, and the verdict is guilty.

This book had its origins in the desire to bring that guilty verdict to the attention of parents, teachers and kids, but somewhere along the way it grew in size and scope to include all the drugs of abuse (see reference section at back). I don't know how I agreed to that, I must have been on something pretty strong at the time. The small six-month project Trevor Grice promised me wound up consuming the best part of three years.

Where the science makes sense and meaning soars into flight, Trevor and I pay homage to the wonderful men and women who work long, unglamorous hours in laboratories on behalf of all of us. Where the facts seem leaden-footed and the information refuses to dance, the blame is Trevor's alone.

Tom Scott
Kilbirnie, Wellington

Mortuaries are the hidden places of society, the dust under the rug of our communities, especially when the deceased are lying there not of natural causes but of suicide or misadventure. I remember vividly my first visit to one: I stood there looking down on this youthful distorted face, a mere boy of some scholastic ability who had been tipped to be a high achiever. The warder had pulled him on the trolley into better light, a cardboard tag was tied to his big toe. His face was frighteningly discoloured, as it had been some days since they found him. No words transpired, just a nod of my head, a signature, and later the facing of his distressed parents, the inevitable coroner's report, the funeral, grief and memories.

Over the next 25 years, because of the nature of my work, I was to identify dozens of young people with similar endings. Frustration, despair and anger would manifest itself, especially when you knew it all started with drug experimentation, then regular

Trevor Grice

THIS CANNABIS EDUCATION RESOURCE BOOKLET WILL HELP TEACHERS HELP PUPILS WORK OUT WHAT LEVEL OF BRAIN DAMAGE IS RIGHT FOR THEM...

use, then regular abuse, and from lesser drugs to greater drugs, and from lesser amounts to greater amounts.

The tragedy of drug use with children and adolescents is that they absorb these substances much faster than adults, the blood level of these drugs will consequently be higher and their effect on the body greater. Their livers metabolise them (break them down into smaller compounds) less efficiently, and their kidneys excrete them (eliminate them from the body) more slowly. At the same time their personality, intellect, and body systems are undergoing profound changes thus rendering them vastly more susceptible to harm than adults, who, in theory anyway, are fully formed and mature.

I hope that this book will empower parents and will help teenagers to delay any decisions about drug use until they have completed maturation. The process of maturation can last seven years from the onset of the first signs.

I have taken considerable inspiration from Pablo Casals, who said:

"Sometimes I look about me with a feeling of complete dismay. In the confusion that afflicts the world today, I see a disrespect for the very values of life.

"Beauty is all around us, but how many are blind to it! They look at the wonder of this earth and seem to see nothing.

"Each second we live is a new and unique moment of the Universe, a moment that will never be again...

"And what do we teach our children? We teach them that two and two make four and that Paris is the capital of France.

"When will we also teach them: Do you know what you are? You are a marvel. You are unique. In all the years that have passed, there has never been another child like you. And look at your body - what a wonder it is. Your legs, your arms, your fingers, the way you move. You may become a Shakespeare, a Michelangelo, a Beethoven. You have the capacity for anything. Yes, you are a marvel. And when you grow up, can you then harm another who is, like you, a marvel? You must cherish one another. You must work - we all must work - to make this world worthy of its children."

We accept that people take mood-altering substances, because they enjoy altering their moods. But there is a low for every high. A return journey for every trip. What every child entering adolescence needs to understand is that there is no short cut to happiness through chemistry. There is just a short circuit of the unique brain wiring that makes them, them.

Trevor Grice
Tararua Ranges

THE CHALLENGE

CHAPTER 1

PUBERTY
BLUES

THE STRESSES AND STRAINS OF ADOLESCENCE

In a perfect world all adolescents would start puberty at the same time – the beginning of the school year would be nice. Puberty would be of fixed duration and all the physical and psychological changes would be synchronised. Adolescence would then be a well-defined, finite, predictable business.

It isn't.

The physiology of adolescence may be the same the world over, but psychologically the path to adulthood has different lengths in different cultures. In the Third World it can be traversed in an afternoon. In the West, if you are a typically impatient teenager, it can seem like an eternity.

Some boys get pimples and sprout hair alarmingly all over their top lip, yet stubbornly remain the same height for ages. They wake up one morning and their voice has dropped, and something else has dropped as well. Some girls sprout hair alarmingly from other regions of their bodies and grow eight inches in eight months, yet spend hours staring anxiously into empty bra cups waiting for things to happen.

Everyone goes through puberty in their own messy, magical way. One of the great wonders of life is that we are all utterly unique. Each of us is constructed from our own special blueprint (our chromosomes), and on that master plan quite distinct parental, cultural, religious and social influences are imprinted.

The onset of puberty is not always easy to spot. Some of the clues are very subtle. A useful signal, however, is the overwhelming urge to look up words like COITUS, GONADS and ORGASM in the dictionary. Children find these definitions easy to locate, as most school dictionaries spring open automatically at the required pages - probably because 25 years earlier their parents were looking up the same words.

> "Adolescence: a stage between infancy and adultery."
>
> *H.L. Mencken*

Curiosity about COITUS, GONADS and ORGASM is one of the early indications that the brain is preparing the body to abandon childhood.

It does this by running a tape measure over the rest of the body, and if all the systems are ready it instructs the pituitary (a special gland at the base of the brain just above the roof of the mouth) to unleash hormones (chemical messengers) that travel in the bloodstream to the gonads (testicles in boys, ovaries in girls) and tell them to start producing sex hormones (testosterone in boys, oestrogen and progesterone in girls).

At this point, all hell breaks loose. Physically, mentally, emotionally and spiritually they will never be the same again.

And the single most common factor for all adolescents moving through this potentially explosive process is stress.

"A father is a banker provided by Nature."

Oxford Book of Aphorisms

◆ **THE STRESS IS PHYSICAL**

Growing extra bone and muscle and beginning to ovulate or produce spermatozoa is a time-consuming, energy-sapping business. Adolescents, like infants, require more sleep in order to recharge the body's electro-chemical systems.

◆ **THE STRESS IS EMOTIONAL**

These startling physical changes, arriving without warning, often cause confusion, disorientation, guilt and panic in the unprepared.

◆ **THE STRESS IS MENTAL**

At the very time their testicles are letting them know they are there, these would-be adults are expected to solve complicated algebra problems and remember the annual rainfall of the Amazon basin. Their breasts throb with pain, yet they are supposed to go into raptures over Shakespeare's sonnets and understand photosynthesis too. Parents and teachers are exhorting them to settle down and concentrate while the rest of their world is topsy-turvy.

Academic pressure from the front of the classroom and at home doesn't always seem that relevant when right alongside you other pupils are changing in all sort of ways - loyalties shift and jealousies emerge as old friends make new friends and you may be left out.

To mature at a different rate is to fall out of step with your contemporaries. Anyone falling behind is open to feelings of abandonment and ridicule. "Nerds" fall behind and are targets for bullying. On the other hand, anyone getting ahead can feel awkward and embarrassed. Finding old friends immature, they are suddenly open to the charge of being "stuck up".

Ahead, behind or perfectly in step, every adolescent in their search for a comfortable identity fears teasing and rejection, has difficulty communicating emotions and can at times feel terribly powerless.

If that weren't bad enough, when children reach adolescence, many parents change for the worse. Overnight they become boring, selfish, insensitive, impatient, intolerant, ignorant, penny-pinching, nagging, suspicious, paranoid, dogmatic, judgmental, vindictive, sneaky, calculating, obsessed with hygiene, obsessed with order, obsessed with possessions, hyper-irritable, hyper-critical, hyper-anxious, over-protective, humourless, conservative, and deeply embarrassing to their children and their children's friends.

Mercifully these symptoms tend to disappear when adolescents complete maturation and move into their late teens. Most parents have fully recovered by the time their children reach their 20s.

IS MY CHILD ON DRUGS?

HOW TO SPOT THE WARNING SIGNS

Given all the tensions and frustrations of adolescence, imagine how a teenager might feel on being handed a substance that when inhaled, ingested or injected is said to make all your hassles vanish. The temptation to experiment is understandably considerable.
So are the risks.

All teenagers are difficult, withdrawn, secretive and utterly self-centred at least some of the time. Teenagers with drug problems are difficult, withdrawn, secretive and utterly self-centred most of the time.

Parents worried about which category their teenager might belong in should rely on their instincts. All parents want to be able to trust their children but that shouldn't mean ceasing to trust your own intuition. Almost without exception, no one knows a child better than its own parents, and almost without exception no one cares about that child more than its own parents.

Of course, children and adolescents using drugs seldom announce this fact to their parents. When asked directly if they are using drugs they will probably deny it angrily or scoff loudly at the mere suggestion. For the sake of a quiet life kids know it's easier to lie to their parents, and for the sake of a quiet life many parents - intuition notwithstanding - are tempted to believe them. Denial is not confined to drug users alone - many parents will go to extraordinary lengths to blind themselves to the obvious.

For some parents the moment of truth is forced on them. Their children's lies collapse of their own accord or there is a knock on the door from the authorities. There is no need, however, to wait nervously for that knock on the door confirming your worst fears - if you know what to look for, even the most secretive and calculating child on drugs will unwittingly provide all the corroborative evidence needed to establish the truth.

The clues range from changes in behaviour to changes in physical appearance. Some of these signs can indicate other medical conditions, but a combination of the ones listed below, especially if they are of recent occurrence, should raise serious questions in parents' minds. Adolescents worried about a brother, sister or friend should look for the same telltale signs.

BEHAVIOURAL CHANGES

♦ Dramatic and unexpected changes in attitude.

♦ Isolation in room for unusual lengths of time.

♦ Habitual lying; will cover one lie with another.

♦ Tardy, delinquent behaviour.

♦ Violence, physical and/or verbal.

♦ Secretive behaviour, such as sneaking away and making excuses about where they are going or where they have been.

♦ Strange and secretive telephone calls.

♦ Shoplifting and stealing; unexplained disappearance of money or valuables (e.g., CDs that can be sold easily) from the family home or friends' homes.

♦ Disregard and disrespect for the values of the home and indifference to other members of the family.

♦ Manipulates parents, one against the other.

♦ Wears sunglasses at inappropriate times.

SCHOOL-RELATED CHANGES

♦ Sudden or gradual drop in school grades and achievement levels.

♦ Working well below their level of ability.

♦ Disrespect, defiance towards teachers, rules and regulations.

♦ Being inattentive in class; difficulty with studying.

♦ Skipping classes, frequent truancy, suspensions.

PHYSICAL CHANGES

♦ Erratic sleeping and eating habits.

♦ Dramatic weight changes, beyond normal weight loss or gain.

♦ Slurred speech.

♦ Burns on hands or clothing.

♦ Constant sniffing, runny eyes and nose; difficulty fighting off colds and infections.

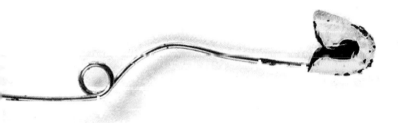

MENTAL AND EMOTIONAL CHANGES

Emotional outbursts, rapid mood swings.

Vagueness about company kept and where time was spent.

♦ Distorted time sense.

Loss of short-term memory.

Shorter attention span.

Exaggerated sensitivity to self; insensitivity to others.

Difficulty concentrating on a single task.

♦ Unreasonable resentments.

SOCIAL CHANGES

Changes in peer group, with little interest in old friends.

Trouble with authority figures and the law.

Seems to have money, but no job.

♦ Has job, but always needs more money.

As for more concrete evidence, alarm bells should definitely ring in your head if you happen to find - usually clumsily hidden - any of the following in your teenager's room: pipes, bongs, plastic bags, rolling papers, seeds, stems, razor blades, mirrors, blackened spoons and knives, small tins, a portable heat source such as a primus, a strange smoky smell in clothing or any other indicators of drug paraphernalia.

And if everything else fails, and suspicion still remains...

TRY THIS SIMPLE TEST:

Devised by a Californian research scientist and treatment specialist, Dr Forrest Tennant, this is a very simple test for suspected teenage marijuana abuse. There are no laboratory tests involved and you can do this in the privacy of your own home.

(By the way, don't let some of the chemical terminology bother you. We're getting to that stuff shortly. Just see if the memory problems sound familiar.)

Here's how Dr Tennant explains the Tennant test:

"If I've got a teenager in my office and I think they're using marijuana, I say, 'I want you to tell me what time you got up yesterday morning'.

"I have them give me the time. Then I ask them, 'What did you do when you got up? What clothes did you put on? What did you eat for breakfast? What time did you go to school? What did you study in

school? What did you watch on TV?' I make them go hour by hour through the day before. If they've lost their acetylcholine they don't know - they can't remember.

"They'll give you the biggest song and dance you ever heard. 'Well, I, you know...I got up. I know I got to school...and I watched TV... and I just hung out.' They'll give you all these vague terms just like an Alzheimer's case. They'll avoid the question.

"Now think about it for just about 10 seconds. You can remember what time you got up yesterday morning. You can probably remember what clothes you put on, what you ate for breakfast, and when you went to work, and what you ate for lunch, and where you went after work, and what you did last night.

"It's not that tough. And just remember, if you can do it, teenagers sure as heck ought to be able to. And if they can't do it, what you've just diagnosed, and what you don't need blood tests to confirm, is acetylcholine deficiency. And that's somebody getting into trouble with marijuana. If they're losing their memory, you've got a big problem in a teenager.

"It's a simple test that doesn't cost any money and is particularly relevant for teenagers, because their reservoirs of neurochemicals are more fragile than adults', and so are their brain receptor sites. They are much more susceptible than adults to probable dependence and damage."

Children and adolescents who fit the above warning signs or fail the Tennant test almost certainly have a problem with substance abuse. But proving that someone has a problem and getting them to do something about it are two different things. It could also be a problem they are not ready to acknowledge - they may argue that their drug-taking is harmless, or that they know the risks and are operating well within what they consider their safety margins.

Forcing people to change their behaviour against their will is ethically questionable and therapeutically dubious. The best solutions to substance abuse problems come when people openly accept they have a problem and choose of their own accord to change their behaviour, which may or may not involve the help and support of others.

This can and does happen - see, for instance, Chapter 8 ("The Story of Two Users", page 41) - and it's proof that self-preservation is a powerful drive in all of us. Even the most zealous anarchist, dedicated to the complete overthrow of the state, drives home from meetings on the correct side of the road. The only people who willingly leap off tall buildings are those who know that the practice is harmful to their health.

But anyone struggling to accept that they have a substance abuse problem would be immeasurably helped if they had some understanding of how their brain

was currently operating, compared with how it used to perform.

Even though we all carry one round in our heads, most of us have scarcely begun to grasp what an incredibly complex, wonderfully responsive, yet terribly fragile instrument the brain is. Every brain is a miraculous tapestry utterly unique to the weaver - and there are no huge looms capable of manufacturing exact replicas. When

"He who is convinced against his will is of the same opinion still."

Proverb

we tear that tapestry we are damaging a one-off that can't be easily - perhaps ever - mended.

In the following chapters we take a closer look at just how the brain works - and the damage that can so easily be done to it. But first, a mother's story.

A MOTHER'S STORY

THE WASTE OF A LIFE

It is just over a year since Emily's death, and the pain is only starting to lift. I had 15 good years with her and three bad ones. I am left with a feeling of futility at the waste of an intelligent, beautiful and artistic little girl's life. I will never see Emily exhibit her art. I'll never see her be a bridesmaid at her sister's wedding, or be a bride herself. I will never hold the grandchildren she would have given me. When I am an old lady she will not be there to hold my hand when I die.

It all started with the beatings at high school. She was still very little and the big kids picked on her. Not that she was blameless - she told me she liked winding people up. The final straw was when she had her nose punched down at the mall by one of the group.

The police were called, and at a family group conference the girl concerned apologised. We thought it was all sussed and we could relax, but by the start of the new school year Emily's behaviour had deteriorated and she became a very different person - telling lies, disobeying all our rules and having big mood swings. Her father and I felt frightened and hopeless. Her new friends were the "bad kids" at school and she said she now felt popular.

I asked Social Welfare for help, but they could only offer me a family group conference in six weeks' time. Our next step was to get an appointment with a psychologist for the whole family, as the whole family was on the receiving end of Emily's behaviour.

That was a big mistake. She only came to one of the four appointments and then she stared at the ceiling the whole time and wouldn't participate at all. Then we discovered "Tough Love" and we felt more in control, even though Emily called us "Mr and Mrs Hitler".

Then the bomb dropped - the school was suspending her for drinking on the school raffle selling day. The headmaster told me they suspected her of dope smoking. That would have certainly explained

> "I found being frightened was a normal everyday feeling."

some of her behaviour and her deteriorating school work. She was overjoyed to be rid of her "dumb school" and went around home laughing. We were all very upset and cried heaps, which made Emily laugh even more. I felt frightened of Emily, something I never thought possible.

The school phoned me to let me know she could come back if she attended counselling, but by this time Emily had run away with her friend Janice. The police were informed she was missing and we spent the next 10 days looking for her. Her friends moved her from place to place, to keep one step ahead of us. When she turned up at home she was dirty, smelly, exhausted, very angry and defiant.

School was due to start again, and as her last school wouldn't have her back, I tried the other two high schools near us. But because she was suspected of smoking dope, neither would have her.

One school said they would take her if she agreed to regular drug testing - she refused, of course. I was dreading having her hanging around home, as she had been

threatening me with violence. I asked a family friend for help. He was associated with a church group that had a girls' hostel, and they took Emily in. She was enrolled at Linwood High School and we were able to settle down a bit ourselves.

Within a short time, though, the same cycle of bad behaviour and dope-using started again with her new schoolfriends. My weight by this time had plummet to seven stone. She started running away again and got taken in by the St Alban's parish and placed with a young couple of schoolteachers. I started to pick up but it was too good to be true: she started playing up and was asked to leave. She sat her School Certificate and got A and B marks. At the end of the year Harry's brother in Auckland invited Emily to go with his family for a North Island tour for four weeks, so off she went.

When she came home she was just like her old self. She enrolled at Hagley High School in five subjects as a sixth-former, even though she was only 15. Her father built her a room of her own. It had new carpet and red velvet curtains chosen by

her. But within a few weeks the bad behaviour started again and Social Welfare were as useless as before. The school counsellor made appointments for us all which we attended but Emily did not.

Emily ran away again several times. With all the money I'd spent on her room, I felt robbed and angry. We reported her missing to the police. After two weeks and a lot of detective work by me, I located her staying with an ex-schoolfriend's family in Redcliffs - she had told them "Mum" had said she could leave home.

I tried to persuade her to come back home but Social Welfare wouldn't back me. She got a part-time job to pay her way, and moved out of that house to live in a flat with her yucky boyfriend. The landlord gave me the creeps. He said he would keep a fatherly eye on her.

By that time she was 16 and able to apply for the independent youth benefit without our consent. We went with her to the interview anyway. The officer was really young, and despite me telling her about Emily's drug-taking she backed Emily. I felt angry and

"Her death was such a small mistake."

EMILY VANESSA BROWN
28·3·1975   11·12·1993
Treasured daughter of HAROLD & LESLEY BROWN
Special little sis of SELENA & ROBERT
YOU CAME INTO OUR LIVES AND LEFT FOOT PRINTS ON OUR HEARTS
Always our Em

helpless. We didn't seem to count. I knew then I had lost all hope of any control. On the way out Emily said, "I'll chuck in my job so I can lie in bed all day."

The landlord kicked her boyfriend out and started supplying her with dope and making passes at her. She left there quickly and ended up in a central city flat that was only fit to be condemned. There was dirt piled up against the walls, there were no floor coverings, everyone slept on mattresses on the floor, and no dishes were ever done. It only cost $40 a week, so there was plenty left over for drugs and alcohol.

She really hit it hard in that flat. Her clothes were dirty too. My beautiful daughter had lost all her soft pretty looks.

I tried Social Welfare and the police again, but had no luck. Her father and I talked to her for the millionth time. Her friends were harder, older addicts. Every night without fail I was awake worrying about her and wondering if there was anything I could do to bring this nightmare to an end.

Often when I visited her she was intoxicated and abusive. The house was freezing in the winter and she slept in her clothes. She asked to come home, so I collected her quickly and brought her and her smelly clothes here. Most of her underwear went into the rubbish tin on the end of a stick. As I wouldn't let her boyfriend doss down in the spare room with her, she got angry and went back to the grotty house. She left on Thursday. On Saturday she rang to say the house had burned down at 10 o'clock that morning and she had escaped by climbing out of a window.

I felt relieved that she was alive and hoped that the bad fright would make her think. She came home and was well-behaved, but was gone again in two weeks.

A series of yucky flats followed, with equally awful people. One house had a large supply of dope growing in the back yard, which I reported to the police, but there was no action taken.

I think it was at that house that she started using prescription pills and/or needles. The deterioration was marked. I challenged her to get into rehab, as did her straight friends. I found being frightened was a normal everyday feeling. She flatted for six months with a boy who had been an addict for years and been in prison several times.

I only went there if asked. They were filthy and so were their clothes, they hardly ate and the dog pooed inside. I increased my visits for the sole purpose of picking up and listing the empty pill bottles lying everywhere. One particular city doctor was involved. I submitted the list to the drug squad, they referred me to the Ministry of Health, and I then made an official complaint. I found another example of one law for doctors and another law for us.

Her health was suffering now and I had no doubt that she was going to die. She came home to us for two weeks, and every day she would disappear for a while - to use, I supposed. She was cleanly clothed and had a clean bed, and she would say, "Mum, I love you helping me be clean here. It feels so nice" - but soon she was gone to another awful flat, with three men who used drugs.

One day when they were out, the house was firebombed. Emily was really scared and put herself into a church home and started going to Narcotics Anonymous meetings. I felt she had turned a corner and I felt good for the first time in years, but late at night two weeks later she rang to say she was moving on and going flatting with her mates, and I was in the depths of despair again.

I didn't hear from her for four weeks - she said she was in a nice clean house, and when she came to see us one lunchtime she was looking the best I had seen her for ages, and my hopes were up again.

The next day when I was sitting on the toilet, I had a visualisation of her death notice in the paper. I told myself that 99 percent of the bad things that we think will happen don't eventuate.

On Saturday 11 December 1993, I arrived back from collecting a newspaper and the police car was at the gate. As the policeman came towards me I just knew. I said, "She is dead, isn't she?"

Even though I was partially prepared, the pain and grief was just as big. Her death was such a small mistake: her drug patches fell off at a rock concert and instead of going straight home to put on new ones she bought an addict's one-day supply of methadone, then when she got home she put on her patches, and the effect was to overdose her at about 6.00am in her sleep.

Our Maori friends helped us and we had Emily at home for people to visit, and many, many people came. It was really great to be able to talk to her about anything without her answering back, and now I knew she was 100 percent drug-free and would never use again. We buried her in Prebbleton country cemetery, next to her grandmother.

- Lesley

HOW THE
BRAIN WORKS

THE MOST ADVANCED COMPUTER ON EARTH

Nature is ruthlessly efficient and economical. There is no wasted effort. if human beings have two kidneys, it's because they don't need three. Similarly, nature goes to the considerable trouble of housing the heart and lungs in a cage of rib and muscle because it deems those organs vital and worthy of protection.

Nature goes even further with the brain, housing it in an imposing fortress, a castle of bone atop a lofty vantage point with good views over the rest of the body and its surrounding terrain. Inside this fortress is 1.5kg of jelly the size of a grapefruit, and wrinkled on the outside like an overgrown walnut. This unspectacular pinky-grey organ is quite possibly the most wondrous creation in the universe.

The brain consists of two kinds of cell: glial and neurons. Glial cells are about 10 times more numerous but only about a tenth of the size and so take up much the same space as neurons. Apart from supplying nutrients to the neurons and helping to dispose of wastes, the glial cells act as ballast - much like the polystyrene bubble packing that surrounds sensitive electronic equipment when you buy it new.

Neurons are the nerve cells that carry impulses (tiny electrical messages). These are the ones that basically do the mental business - and there are at least 100 billion of them, all capable of making as many as 10,000 connections each. There could be as many as 100 trillion connections in a single brain. More 'bits' than any computer yet dreamed of.

It has been estimated that were we able to build a computer of this complexity and sophistication it would have to be housed in a building 80 storeys high and cover an area the size of Texas. Even assuming there was enough hydro-electricity in the United States and Canada to

> "If the brain was so simple we could understand it, we would be so simple that we couldn't."
>
> *- Lyall Watson*

"So far, the most advanced computer on earth can't duplicate a four-year-old's language ability. It can't even build a bird's nest."

Judith Hooper & Dick Teresi
The 3-Pound Universe

run such a machine it might still be no smarter than your average cocker spaniel.

The 100 billion neurons that make up the hardware in the human brain took over a million years to evolve. 100 billion neurons at birth still only leaves you with a stone age brain. But this stone age brain, when exposed to the twentieth century, rapidly matures into a twentieth century brain.

Other organs mature by growing in size - under instruction from the brain. There is no difference between an adult's heart and an infant's heart - the former is merely a larger version of the latter. It is the same for bone and muscle. However an adult's brain is markedly more complicated than its infant version.

There is a comparable number of neurons but there are vastly more connections. Many of the most important connections are made during maturation (the process of shifting from childhood into young adulthood).

In order to hold a single thought for just a fraction of a second, millions of neurons have to simultaneously connect. They make contact with each other through projections called axons - which meet but don't quite touch. (See Hard Science page 103.) The tiny gap separating each neuron from its neighbour is called a synapse. Information is carried down the axons electrically and across synapses chemically. These chemicals are

"A hundred billion neurons, a hundred trillion connections - that's more than enough to contain a soul."

Judith Hooper, Dick Teresi
The 3-Pound Universe

called neurotransmitters. This place where electricity and chemistry meet is the site of drug action.

Put it another way. Electrical impulses in the brain are like runners in a 4x400 relay - they cover long distances at great speed. Neurotransmitters are like the batons exchanged between the runners. Our brains exchange "batons" when transmitting the signals needed to process inform ation, regulate emotions and keep us alive. Neurotransmitters make us think, feel and act. Drug taking quite literally has heavy users dropping the baton and pulling out of the race.

When neuroscience was in its infancy it was assumed that there was only one neurotransmitter. Over the next 50 years dozens more were discovered - and in the past five years a new one seems to have been discovered every month. Some scientists predict that there could be more than 2000 of them in the brain.

Neuroscience would be a lot simpler if God had settled for just two neurotransmitters. By the same token, a piano with only two keys would be easier to play, but it would not be capable of the infinite variety of melodies available from a standard keyboard.

At a microscopic level the brain is an astonishingly elastic structure. Every skill we acquire, every memory we store, is the result of new connections - and the brain makes new connections in seconds and new nerve pathways in minutes. In fact, as long as it is stimulated properly, it goes on making new connections right up until death.

The brain you have after learning a new language is different from the brain you had before. The brain you have after witnessing a jumbo jet crash in flames in a crowded shopping mall is different from the brain you had just seconds before. Life changes our brains all the time.

It changes them even as they are being formed in the foetus. The 10,000 or so interconnections that every neuron is capable of making begin in the womb, enabling every new-born baby to breathe, eat, excrete and recognise its mother at the very least.

It doesn't remain a mere mammary docking module for very long, however. The connections increase dramatically over the next few years as the child learns to walk and talk. There is another "population explosion" of connections as the child enters adolescence and maturation.

Poets tell us that adolescence is springtime - leaf and blossom appear, and vines burgeon with the promise of fruit to come.

The reality is not so innocent and simple: beneath the surface there is din and clamour as the brain

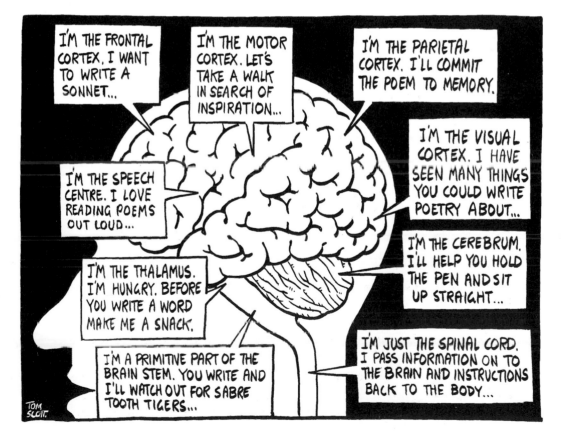

reinvents itself, then reinvents the body. No audible sounds emerge from this secret electro-chemical world as it transforms child into adolescent and adolescent into adult.

Imagine the largest stock exchange that ever existed at opening time during a bull market. 100 billion dealers are buying, selling and exchanging shares making deals, cancelling deals, off-loading old plant, investing in new plant, recording information, analysing information, discarding redundant information, permanently storing vital information, anticipating market trends, and making split-second decisions, like whose turn it is to make the coffee.

Brain activity is something like that - and it's all mute. The mental trading is done with nods, winks and subtle signs. Chemicals move in and out of nerve cells, and tiny electrical currents whizz up and down nerve pathways. All thinking, feeling and acting is a consequence of the 100 billion cells doing deals with each other.

Any foreign substance that interrupts the nods, winks and subtle signs retards or impairs this secondary evolution of the brain, robbing a child of its full potential. The consequences can be very devastating - the equivalent of a Wall Street crash.

A QUIET DAY IN THE SECONDARY EVOLUTION OF THE BRAIN...

THE LATEST WORD ON HOW THE BRAIN MATURES

Turning 21 was once a much bigger deal in this part of the world than it is today. In fact, just about every dusty town and hamlet in Australia and New Zealand had a shop or two selling mirrors cut into the shape of keys with the magic number, '21', emblazoned on them. On the big night proud parents presented these keys to the birthday boy or birthday girl to symbolise the opening of the door to adulthood. Turning 21 meant more back then because you couldn't vote or drink on licensed premises until you reached this age. With the lowering of the voting and drinking age to 18, turning 21 has less social significance today, and mirrors cut into the shape of keys seem quaint and faintly silly now.

The latest MRI (magnetic resonance imaging) studies of children's and teenagers' brains confirm that our parents' and grandparents' generations weren't far off the mark in selecting 21 as the cut-off point for adolescence. Using these scans scientists have been able to map the extensive structural changes as they occur in the brains of young people, from the onset of puberty right up until the age of 25 - although no one in their right mind would want to institute a big tradition of 25th birthday parties! What they found was that the brain grows very little over the course of childhood. By the time a child reaches six the brain is about 90 percent of its adult size. Between the ages of six and twelve the brain undergoes a growth spurt and increases in volume. It does this not through the creation of new neurons but through the vast proliferation of connections or synapses between neurons. In essence the brain lays

> I envy people who take drugs—at least they know what to blame everything on.
>
> *Anon.*

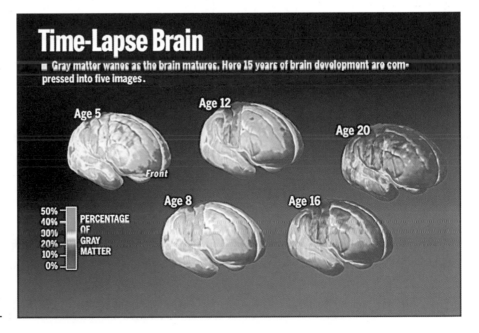

Time-Lapse Brain

■ Gray matter wanes as the brain matures. Here 15 years of brain development are compressed into five images.

Age 5
Age 12
Age 20
Front
Age 8
Age 16

50%
40%
30%
20%
10%
0%

PERCENTAGE OF GRAY MATTER

far more cabling and wiring than it eventually needs. If you think of the brain as a sprawling mansion, it doesn't add on any more wings during adolescence it just puts multiple high-speed internet connections into every room, including the toilets, linen cupboards, broom closets and pantries - in places it probably doesn't really need them, but it's ready for everything. The thickening of the neurones and their branch-like dendrites - the brain's grey matter - peak when girls are about eleven and boys about thirteen, at which point selective pruning begins.

As teenagers learn who they are and what they want to become their brains trim back the number of synapses in a process that has run its course by about the age of 25. At the same time there is an increase in the fatty insulation, myelin sheaths, around neurons - the brain's white matter - which protects and strengthens the electric impulses being sent between neurons. During adolescence the brain opts for fewer but faster connections. Raw, wide-ranging potential for learning is traded-off against individual skills and a unique take on the world.

People change their brains as their brains are changing them. Studies show that practising the piano quickly thickens neurons in regions of the brain that control the fingers. Other studies show that London cab drivers who must memorise all the streets of that city have an unusually large hippocampus, a structure involved in storing and retrieving knowledge.

MRI scans reveal that the waxing and waning of grey matter as the brain matures proceeds in stages, generally from the back to the front. Some of the brain regions that reach maturity first - through proliferation and subsequent pruning - are those in the back of the brain and these mediate direct contact with the environment through sensory functions such as vision, hearing, touch and spatial processing. The very last part of the brain to be pruned and shaped to its adult dimensions is the prefrontal cortex, home of the so-called executive functions - planning, setting priorities, organising thoughts, suppressing impulses, and weighing the consequences of one's actions. In short, the part of the brain that

makes teenagers become responsible is the last to mature.

By this time hormones have already been raging out of control for a couple of years. At puberty the ovaries and testes begin to pour oestrogen and testosterone into the bloodstream. The sex hormones are especially active in the brain's emotional centre - the limbic system - creating an appetite for thrills, strong sensations and excitement. Some argue that this thrill seeking evolved to cut parental bonds and encouraged them to leave the family nest and explore the wider world to find their own path and partner. In the modern world where fast cars, illicit drugs, gangs and dangerous liaisons beckon, it also puts the teenager at risk!

Regions of the brain that shy away from dangerous impulsive behaviour are still under construction, while regions of the brain responsible for things like sensation-seeking and risk-taking have their foot to the floor. In short, for quite some time the teenage brain is all accelerator and no brake.

VANDALISM IN THE REFINERY

WHAT DRUGS CAN DO TO THE BRAIN

Until recently, no one knew quite why chewing the leaves of a small shrub found growing high in the Andes gave the chewer a sudden rush of energy. Or why licking the skin of a certain species of tropical toad caused hallucinations. Or why igniting the leaves of some plants and then inhaling the smoke elevated your mood.

The short answer to all of the above is that there are thousands of chemicals in nature with properties similar to the brain's own mood-altering chemicals.

When these naturally occurring chemicals are ingested or inhaled they enter the bloodstream and travel to the central nervous system, where they mimic, or inhibit, the actions of the brain's own mood-altering chemicals.

The greatest manufacturer and user of mood-altering chemicals on the planet is the human brain. Every second of your life, your brain is manufacturing its own drugs, distributing its own drugs, dealing its own drugs and consuming its own drugs. These are the neurotransmitters.

The brain's own drug factories are located at the end of axons. Although the amount of neurotransmitters needed at each synapse is minuscule, there's upwards of 100,000,000,000,000 synapses to service, so the brain's own drug tab to itself adds up.

Many central nervous system disorders are caused by imbalances in the functioning of neurotransmitters or from a deficiency in the specific nutrients needed for their manufacture.

In extreme emotional states such as schizophrenia, rage, terror or despair, the brain is virtually overdosing on some of its own drugs. In other states, such as Parkinson's disease and suicidal depression, the brain is virtually going

> "A drug is a substance that when injected into a guinea pig produces a scientific paper."
>
> *L & M Cowan,*
> ***The Wit of Medicine***

through withdrawal as it runs out of certain neurotransmitters. Fasting and malnutrition will limit the quantity of neurotransmitters that the brain can replenish. So will sleep deprivation.

Some neurotransmitters, such as the endorphins - feel-good chemicals - have become stars in their own right and have entered the popular consciousness. The most humble weekend jogger is now able to proudly defend his painful-looking shuffle on the grounds that endorphins are giving him a runner's high.

Long before endorphins were discovered, scientists postulated that if chewing opium leaves made people feel good, then the brain itself must have naturally occurring opiate receptors and naturally occurring opiates triggering them. Blood tests confirm that aerobic exercise, sex, laughter, listening to a favourite piece of music, or listening to a good preacher, a good therapist or a good coach, are all capable of raising endorphin levels.

In one sense our brains are little more than vast refinery complexes filled with tanks, vats and reservoirs of transmitters. Our thoughts, feelings and acts are governed to some extent by which vats are filled to overflowing and which reservoirs are close to empty. Mood-altering drugs work by indiscriminately puncturing and draining the various vats and reservoirs.

When transmitter tanks are drained, supplies have to be built up again from dietary amino acids. People who consume huge quantities of noradrenalin by expending

We understand how folk medicine worked with plants. People were eating plants anyway. They noticed that some of them tasted good, some of them made them sick, and some of them made them want to lie around all day listening to the Doors through headphones. *James Gorman, The Man With No Endorphins*

physical energy, concentrating hard on intellectual tasks or by taking stimulants rarely declare "Jeez, I could go a huge feed of tyrosine and phenylalanine" (the dietary amino acids needed by the brain to manufacture noradrenalin). Instead, they reach for more stimulants, which only further depletes the tanks - slowly, in the case of a cup of coffee; a lot more quickly in the case of substance abuse.

A HEALTHY INDIVIDUAL CAN KEEP ALL OF HIS OR HER NEUROTRANSMITTER TANKS TOPPED UP BY:

♦ *Maintaining a nutritious diet rich in vitamins, including the 10 essential amino acids in children and eight essential amino acids in adults, and the lecithin and choline needed to make the neurotransmitter acetylcholine.*

♦ *Avoiding chronic stress, such as the permanent pain of rheumatoid arthritis or chronic migraine - chronic stress depletes tank levels.*

♦ *Getting a decent night's sleep. It is during sleep that the body manufactures and replenishes the transmitters - which is why sleep deprivation is the basis of brainwashing. The tank levels go down and defiance rapidly becomes compliance. Even broken sleep can profoundly alter moods, as the parents of newborn babies know only too well. After five nights of interrupted sleep, a parent who graduated with honours in the sensitivity section at pre-natal class can become a snarling selfish monster.*

Some clinicians say we shouldn't call anybody a marijuana or heroin addict or an alcoholic: we should really say that they are suffering from a neurotransmitter deficiency syndrome.

If an individual's vats containing the chemicals responsible for calm and moderation are nearly empty, and at the same time the vats containing the chemicals responsible for irritation and rage are full, the chances of their responding sensibly to a minor setback or mild confrontation are that much more remote. The response is more likely to be disproportionately aggressive.

Look around you. Our television screens, newspapers and radios are filled with stories of crimes that leave us wondering what drove this or that person to commit some

unspeakable act. Neuroscience is increasingly providing some of the clues.

A number of studies have found, for instance, that people with a history of violent behaviour have lower than usual serotonin levels in the brain. Serotonin is a neuro-transmitter involved in nerve pathways responsible for self-esteem, appetite control and memory among other things.

The human male - the most needlessly aggressive animal on the planet, particularly between the ages of 15 and 25 as road toll statistics attest, has the highest blood levels of the hormone testosterone. And testosterone carried in the bloodstream to the brain is a mood-altering substance that raises libido as it lowers serotonin levels. Nature cruelly heightens libido in young men and makes them giddy with sexual longing at the very time it deprives them of the confidence to do anything about it.

Despite the vast array of neurotransmitters operating in the brain, and the vast array of substances that can mimic or contradict their function, there is a terrible sameness in the language of substance abusers. The same themes repeat themselves and we should take them at their word:

"I got plastered."

"I got legless."

"I got pissed as a chook."

"I got shit-faced."

"I got off my face."

"I got high."

"I got stoned."

"I got zonked."

"I got totally out of it."

"I got blown away."

"I got ripped."

"I got smashed."

"I got blasted."

"I got wasted."

THERE IS A CLEAR PATTERN HERE:

1. Users have difficulty expressing themselves.
2. Demolition is a recurring motif. This is no accident: unwittingly they are describing exactly what is happening to their own neurons.

Analogies do not constitute proof, but they can be useful. If for a moment you imagine the human brain as a shopping mall, alcohol and solvent abuse could be likened to young punks strolling casually through the arcade shattering every plate-glass window with a length of pipe.

Cocaine and heroin are urban guerrillas who toss Molotov cocktails into the entranceway. Loud explosions rock the building. Alarms squeal, sprinklers gush and there is general pandemonium.

Lysergic acid diethylamide (LSD) is a demented graffiti artist with delusions of genius who sprays preposterous images in fantastic colours across every surface. At first glance you can't tell door from window, or floor from ceiling.

Marijuana is a cat burglar. It enters the mall quietly, finds the shop responsible for memory, picks the lock, deactivates the alarm systems and slips inside. Once there, it unscrews the back of every piece of electronic equipment in the place and starts snipping leads and wires at random. It exits just as stealthily, leaving no trace. In the morning everything looks okay but nothing works properly.

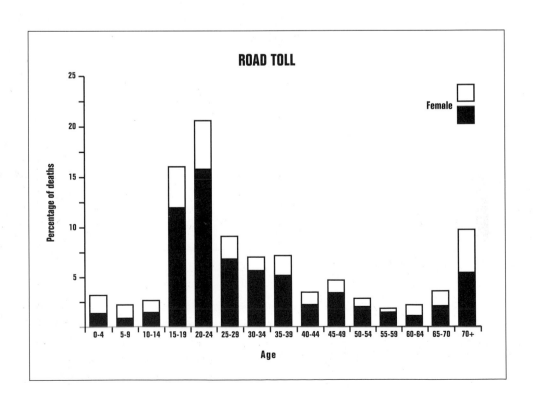

YOU MUST REMEMBER THIS

DRUGS AND MEMORY LOSS

All of what we know about the world that went before us, the world we live in now and our particular place in it - all of that, we have had to learn.

Learning is the process by which we acquire new knowledge. Memory is the process by which we retain that knowledge over time.

The actual mechanics of how and where memories are made and stored has been the subject of much scientific debate. The precise details are still being hotly contested but there is broad acceptance that when you learn something new the information is somehow etched into your cerebral circuitry at incredible speed.

A unique pattern of neurons is quickly forged together - and if exposure to the event is repeated, and the event itself is significant, the constellation of synapses will be strengthened.

Memory is the steady, yet selective accumulation of the present. What is happening to you right now will become memory just a few seconds later. Learning and memory are central to our sense of individuality, and loss of memory leads to loss of contact with one's immediate self, one's life history and other human beings.

All incoming sensory information - from sight, sound, taste, touch, smell - goes to a critically important clearing-house in the brain called the hippocampus, which helps convert immediate experience into short-term memory and short-term memory into

> ## "Sticks and stones may break my bones, but names will never hurt me."
>
> *The sentiments of the "Sticks and Stones" homily are noble but the reverse is true. Physical pain, while uncomfortable at the time, is usually quickly forgotten, whereas insults can burn themselves into our memories like branding irons. They can keep us awake at night years later, and in extreme cases we take them fresh and vivid to our graves.*

> # "I think, therefore I am."
>
> *- Rene Descartes*

permanent memory.

The hippocampus is particularly susceptible to damage from many mood-altering substances. A diminished hippocampus leads to diminished memory. Making sense of the immediate past becomes difficult. Making sense of the immediate future is problematic too.

In severe cases people can be trapped permanently in the present, which in essence is what happens with Alzheimer's disease.

"The one good thing about Alzheimer's is that you're always meeting new people".

Alzheimer's sufferer Ronald Reagan

In "Strawberry Fields Forever" John Lennon sang that "nothing is real". If you are in a philosophical frame of mind and it's late at night and you've endured a pretty meaningless sort of day this proposition has considerable appeal. If, however, you strike your thumb with a mallet at this juncture it becomes exceedingly difficult to sustain the notion that reality is just a figment of the imagination.

Reality is what we are experiencing now - measured against what we already know and what we expect the world to be.

People don't usually take drugs with the single intention of losing all contact with their immediate reality - unless of course they are desperately tired, in which case they can take sleeping pills.

People take drugs to modify and enhance their immediate relationship with reality. Like every other experience you've ever had, this altered perception of reality is duly recorded, if only temporarily, in the memory.

All that you experience, even altered perceptions of reality, has to be sorted and ordered by the hippocampus. Important experiences are set aside for permanent storage. Seeing a jumbo jet crashing into a shopping mall would come into this category. Other experiences are either placed in the "matters pending" tray or shredded within hours. Remembering what side of the handbasin you placed your toothbrush this morning would come into the latter category. Remembering where you put the car keys the night before comes somewhere between matters pending and shred immediately.

The key to all learning, be it a poem you are trying to memorize or a new skill you would like to acquire, is repetition. When the "matters pending" tray is filled to overflowing with the same

Images of faces, the plots of a thousand novels and movies, the way bacon tastes and coffee smells - how do we remember all these things? And where does our memory reside? We can hear a melody for only a few seconds and yet carry it with us for a lifetime. Experience somehow leaves its mark on the mind. But how can something as fleeting as song take on substance and become part of the brain, part of the body? How do we carry the past around in our heads?

George Johnson,
In the Palaces of Memory

experiences, the brain takes the hint and stores the information long-term. A circuit left unused will eventually unravel, and attempted reactivation will retrieve a rough and faded memory at best.

By repeatedly taking mood-altering chemicals and repeatedly altering your perception of reality you start to store debased memories, and the process of losing contact with your immediate self is set in motion.

Accumulating debased drug memories is serious enough: even worse is that some mood-altering chemicals continue to debase memory and learning well after the particular "high, fix, hit" or what-have-you has worn off. If the mood-altering chemicals permanently damage the hippocampus, then memory and learning is permanently impaired.

THE BRAIN OF R.B.

R.B., a retired Southern California postal worker, in the aftermath of a coronary bypass operation suffered a sudden loss of blood to his brain. Though he survived with most of his faculties intact, he lost his ability to remember. He could recall events that had happened in the years before the operation, but he could not form new memories.

When R.B. died in 1983, his last half-decade an amnesiac blur, three scientists were allowed to dissect and study his brain...

R.B.'s amnesia had not been caused by massive or even moderate brain damage, they discovered, but by a tiny lesion in the hippocampus.

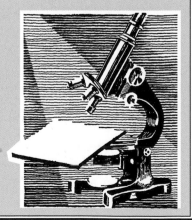

George Johnson,
In the Palaces of Memory

WHAT IS MARIJUANA?

THE FACTS ABOUT CANNABIS *

Marijuana comes from the Cannabis sativa plant, which can be grown easily in warm and temperate climates anywhere in the world. It grows wild on the roadside in Kathmandu, and can be cultivated hydroponically at the South Pole.

In ancient times its fibre was used to make clothing and rope, and for many centuries cannabis was used widely throughout Asia, the Middle East and North Africa as a medicine, as well as for its psychoactive properties.

The plant is tough, and particularly resistant to insects and disease. One way to get rid of it, though, is to turn it on itself: resin taken from the stem and injected into the root system will kill the whole plant.

Unique to *Cannabis sativa* are the resinous substances found in the stem, leaves and flower heads - the 62 cannabinoids. The most active,

"Frequent marijuana use leads to more tissue destruction and long-term impairment of our highest intellectual functions than almost any other drug of abuse."

- Robert Gilkeson, former director Brain Research Centre, California

* See also the entry under MARIJUANA in the reference section, which covers the same ground as this chapter but in fuller and more scientific detail.

the most studied and the one that occurs in the highest concentration is the psychoactive agent Delta-9 tetrahydrocannabinol, commonly known as THC. This is the mood-altering chemical ingredient that induces mild euphoria, relaxation, time distortion and an intensification of ordinary sensory experiences.

"Today's joint could be anywhere between five and 50 times more potent than its 1960s predecessor."

CANNABIS CAN ALSO PRODUCE THE FOLLOWING:

ACUTE SIDE EFFECTS

♦ Reddening of the whites of the eyes.

♦ Dry throat.

♦ Heightened appetite (the "munchies").

♦ Anxiety, panic and paranoia, especially in naive users.

♦ Impairment of short-term memory, concentration span and psychomotor function, increasing the risk of an accident if you drive a vehicle or operate machinery when stoned.

♦ Possible psychotic symptoms such as hallucinations.

CHRONIC SIDE EFFECTS

♦ Probable respiratory diseases.

♦ Possible cannabis addiction.

♦ Memory damage and decline in other intellectual skills.

♦ Increased risk of cancer of aerodigestive tract.

♦ Increased risk of developing schizophrenia.

♦ Increased risk of leukemia and birth defects in the children of women who used cannabis during their pregnancy.

♦ Marked decline in occupational performance in adults, and educational underachievement in children.

♦ Reduced output of reproductive hormones, leading to impaired ovulation, sperm production and libido.

♦ Lower white blood cell production and impaired immune system.

The concentration of THC varies between the three common forms of cannabis available on the market:

Marijuana is prepared from the dried flowering tops and leaves of the harvested plant. Potency depends on growing conditions and the genetic characteristics of the plant: THC concentration can range from 0.5 to 5 percent. (Sinsemilla - marijuana - made just from flower heads - may have from seven to 14 percent.)

Hashish, made from dried cannabis resin and compressed flowers, has a THC concentration ranging from two to 20 percent.

Hash oil, a dark, highly potent, viscous substance is obtained by extracting THC from hashish or marijuana with an organic solvent and concentrating the filtered extract. The THC concentration ranges from 15 to a staggering 50 percent.

Given that users may mix all three forms together, trying to compute the strength of an average dose is a thankless task. All that can be said with any certainty is that over the past 30 years the selective breeding of hybrid varieties of *Cannabis sativa* has increased THC concentrations in the leaves and flower heads to the point where today's joint could be anywhere between five and 50 times more potent than its 1960s predecessor.

When parents exclaim, "Hey, I used to smoke the stuff all the time when I was at university, and look at me, I've got a law degree", they are talking about a substantially different plant. Back in 1969, if you wanted to take in the same amount of THC as today's users regularly inhale, you'd have had to suck on a joint the length of an axe handle.

Marijuana is a widely used illicit drug in many Western countries. Surveys typically report that just over half of all males and about a third of all females have tried it. Usage is highest in young men aged between 15 and 24.

The most common way to absorb it is by smoking. Used orally, THC may take more than an hour to enter the bloodstream, but it is more potent and longer-acting. Upon inhalation, it enters the bloodstream in minutes, and may be active in the nervous system long after it ceases to be detectable in the blood.

THC moves easily into the membranes surrounding every cell in the body. In pregnant women, it slips across the placental barrier and into the foetal bloodstream. Likewise in breastfeeding mothers THC crosses easily into breast milk.

In high concentrations THC molecules clog cell membranes, making it difficult for nutrients to enter and for other substances to move out. This inevitably tends to lower cellular metabolic efficiency - i.e., the way the machine of the body runs. Less efficient cells in the testes produce less of the hormone testosterone, which in turn lowers sperm count and sex drive. Less efficient cells in the cerebral cortex make people less smart. Less efficient cells in the cerebellum make them less physically coordinated. Less efficient cells in the hippocampus mean a poorer memory.

THC's anti-nausea properties, useful in some clinical circumstances, can be fatal when combined with alcohol. Teenagers who smoke a joint or two and also drink heavily suppress their vomiting reflex and imbibe alcohol in quantities that would normally make them ill. Excessive blood alcohol results in uncontrolled anaesthesia, which can end in coma or death.

Growing old, feeble and infirm is part of life, and in the normal course of events it should take you a

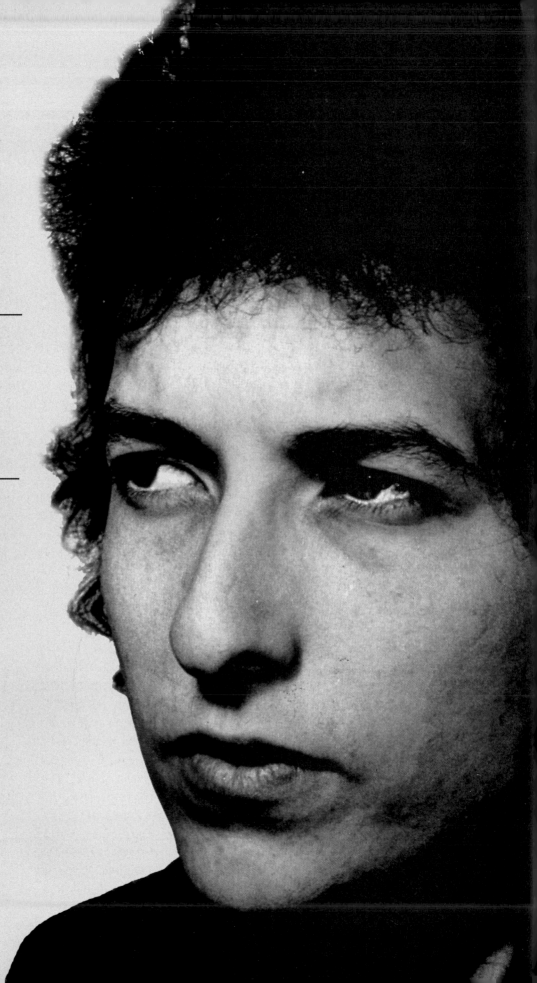

"He not busy
being born is
busy dying".

Bob Dylan

lifetime to get there. Sir William Paton, Professor of Pharmacology at Britain's Oxford University, found brain atrophy in youthful heavy marijuana users equivalent to people aged 70 to 90.

To date, clear-cut, quantitative neuro-anatomical evidence of brain ageing in the hippocampus has been found in connection with chronic exposure to only one drug of abuse - and that is THC.

A growing number of scientific studies have confirmed the detrimental effect of THC - see the entry under MARIJUANA in the reference section. It is important to deal here, however, with one particular argument commonly used in defence of marijuana.

MARIJUANA AS MEDICINE

In ancient times marijuana was used to treat a variety of illnesses, and today many marijuana users swear by its healing powers. Throughout the past two decades there has been strong and growing political pressure on American state and federal legislatures and on the DEA (Drug Enforcement Agency) to reschedule natural marijuana as a medicine.

Despite this clamour for change, the American Medical Association, the American Cancer Society, the American Academy of Ophthalmology, the National Multiple Sclerosis Society and the Food and Drug Administration all state that marijuana has not been found to be an effective and safe medicine, and petitions to reschedule marijuana have failed.

The process by which drugs are approved begins with studies of their chemistry, pharmacology and toxicology. A potential drug has to undergo rigorous clinical trials to test safety and efficacy - first in animals, then in human volunteers and later in patients.

The immediate difficulty with marijuana is that it is not a pure substance - every plant is different. Marijuana is an unstable, varying, complex mixture of more than 400 chemicals, many of which are unstudied either alone or in reaction to each other.

To avoid these complications a prescription drug called Marinol, made of synthetic THC, was approved by the Food and Drug Administration in 1985 as an anti-emetic agent (anti-nausea drug) for chemotherapy patients. In 1992 it was given further approval as an anti-anorexic agent for patients with Aids wasting syndrome.

Because of serious side effects, however, prescription Marinol comes with an information sheet warning that: *"Marinol is highly abusable and can produce both physical and psychological dependence, hallucinations, depression, panic, paranoia. It causes decrements in cognitive performance and memory, decreased ability to control drives and impulses, and impaired co-ordination. Persons using the drug are instructed to be closely supervised by a responsible individual and not to engage in any activities requiring sound judgement. A full-blown psychosis may occur in patients receiving doses within the lower portion of the therapeutic range."*

And that's just the synthetic variety. If all actual cannabis offered for sale in school playgrounds or all joints passed around at parties came with the same warning, doubtless there would be nowhere near as many takers.

THE STORY OF TWO USERS

"WE KNEW WE WERE SICK"

We started using drugs in the third form. At first it was just casually, for the usual reasons - curiosity, experimentation, rebellion. We believed that if we smoked drugs and drank in excess we weren't conforming.

To us that was what we were - rebels, non-conformists. We wanted to be different. Everything we could do to not conform, we did. At our school they pushed hard for conformity, e.g., everyone played rugby. The boarding masters sometimes forced us to do weights so we would play better rugby. As we were boarders we had constant pressure to conform 100 percent of the time.

It was very boring at the boarding school so we needed to do things a little on the "naughty" side to keep our spirits raised. The thrill of almost getting caught, or getting caught and being caned, then telling our girlfriends how sore our arses were - these were our main sources of entertainment.

When we started smoking dope, drugs were cool, we were respected and we felt different. Probably this was our goal - to feel different. We would get our drugs from the gangs and we made contact with a powerful couple who were known in the supplying world.

After beginning drugs we went downhill quite quickly. We wagged school to get stoned and stole money from our parents and friends, or conned other students out of their money to get stoned and out of it. We felt we were doing everything at 110 percent.

We smoked every joint as though it would be our last - every toke would be as hard and long as we could make it. We used as much dope as we could get in the shortest period of time. We never saved any for after but we always managed to get enough money a few hours later, or met someone who we knew would stake us (our speciality). Our wanting to do schoolwork was

> "We knew our parents were emotional wrecks... Thinking back, this part makes us feel sick."

gone and we couldn't remember yesterday's lessons anyway.

We worshipped people like Bob Marley, Robert Plant and Jimmy Page, whom we believed smoked more dooby faster and harder than anyone else. We thought that if you got high enough you would "break through" and be enlightened, be given knowledge and special power. This is what we thought had happened to Led Zeppelin. We got so involved in the music that we started believing that we were the next Robert Plant and the second Jimmy Page. If only we could get high enough, we could be it - do it.

After a while we started having secret lives. We would have places that we could go and get stoned where no-one else could go, and we had a couple of user girlfriends we wouldn't let anyone meet. We started tripping LSD with them and taking a few pills. When this started happening we would try to learn each other's inner secret thoughts.

We became renowned for our lifestyle. If people our age and their parents hadn't met us, then they had almost certainly heard stories. In the dormitory there were three of us - Jeremy, Bart and Ben. Ben, at this time anyway, never got into drugs or even cigarettes seriously. We thought we were the energy of the dormitory. We started school jargon - cool things to say, which other students made part of their vocabulary. We would giggle and laugh and talk at night till we dropped asleep. Generally we would have about two or three hours' sleep a night.

Things started to get really bad and we began to feel paranoid. We had different alibi systems, and our parents kept bugging us, along with the police. We left boarding school on a very bad note. Jeremy was sent to Palmerston North and Bart was sent to Masterton. We kept in contact by phone. We were fairly loyal to each other and we both enjoyed the limelight and the newborn freedom we had, being able to break free from the negative remarks and rules we faced from the school and our families.

We would meet other crazy people who told us we were amazing and really worth getting to know. Though separated, we supported each other, and our energy was being poured into the drug lifestyle. When stoned we felt we could laugh anywhere, do anything, any time. Others thought we were pretty cool, with great stories to tell. Some of our friends started using because they thought we were fun. Some asked us to take them to one of the places in our stories to try drugs with us - the top of Mt Victoria, or the museum and other places. This hurts us a lot now when we think about it. We knew our memories were affected and it was embarrassing when we told lies and couldn't remember.

When we were at school we ran away, and when we left we would run away from home. We both had our own reasons - but we think the bottom line was that we knew we were sick and getting sicker of what was happening around us. When we were caught and taken back home we were angry at being caught but happy that something might happen. Neither of us could see a future.

By this time we were getting stoned every single day. The police referred us to a counsellor. We both went to see the counsellor, and were very interested, but we

Carrington Briggs cared not two figs,
whether he lived or died.
But when he was dead he sat on his bed,
and he cried, and he cried, and he cried.

Spike Milligan

still wanted to have fun and we were set in our ways. We knew our parents were emotional wrecks. Our relationships with our parents and families deteriorated completely. We almost never talked without fighting. Thinking back, this part makes us feel sick.

Gradually we had lost all our fun. Our spirits were low. Even talking to each other on the phone was hard. We felt troubled. We were always troubled with something, we couldn't concentrate on anything and we always felt tired. We had to pump ourselves up to have any energy at all. Any spirit we did have was false. We decided the scientific information the counsellor had given us was right, and we knew we had to try and give up using.

After we had given up for a while, we went back to the counsellor to see if he would help us stay on track. He seemed so pleased and positive when we met him, and we got a natural high about the feelings of hope he gave us.

After a period we started to notice things we hadn't seen for ages, feeling things we hadn't felt in years. We felt high on freedom from drugs and we agreed it was like being stoned - the new freedom.

After a further period we started experiencing withdrawals, depression about not being able to do anything with our lives. We did nothing for months, then finally through the counsellor we found employment.

Sometimes we met people we did drugs with, and when we told them we were clean of everything, they would smile and say "Yeah."

We felt we had finally broken through and finished the drug journey, and were now the guru old men of drugs. We feel we are winning - we have jobs, we are saving, there are no more lies and no more false bullshit. We have formed normal relationships with our parents and friends. We have restarted our lives and are getting back some of the magic feelings that are a much better buzz.

- Bart and Jeremy

CHAPTER 9

SO WHO'D BE A PARENT?

WHEN KIDS PUSH THE LIMITS

When parents learn that their children are taking drugs their initial reactions include guilt, anger, shame, shock and disbelief. Someone has to be responsible - preferably not them. Along with blaming each other they often take issue with the informer and blame the school, a former spouse, the football coach, law enforcement agencies, society at large or the government of the day for good measure.

At the centre of this emotional whirlwind, parents feel isolated and alone. This isolation often contrasts with their children's position. Children taking drugs as part of a group openly discuss the difficulties they are having with parents and swap strategies on how to deal with them.

A popular device is to transfer responsibility back onto the adults:

"My old man is hassling me about a harmless joint, and while he's ranting and raving he has a glass of alcohol in his hand."

"My old lady is always arguing and fighting - I just want peace, man, so I get out of it."

"My parents never listen, it's one-way traffic man, so I just get wasted."

"Parents can talk - what's wrong with us having a few tokes when adults have stuffed up the planet anyway?"

There is just enough truth in the above remarks to make parents feel uncomfortable. The best defence against this sort of pre-emptive strike is education. Parents can't afford to be diverted from the issue of the dangers of drug abuse by the shrewd smokescreens thrown up by their adolescent children.

Ideally that education begins with parents providing a good example to their children. Minors do not have the right to misuse legal substances or use illegal substances, because their parents or caregivers pour themselves a good stiff gin at the end of the day.

All families have their rows - especially when adolescents are around - and today in single-parent homes or homes where both parents work, there never seems to be enough time for roundtable family discussions.

But when children get involved with drugs, parents have to find the time.

Adolescence is a time of experimentation, and most youngsters will push the limits to see how far they can go. A little rebellion can be healthy - but they have to know that some things are unacceptable and will not be tolerated.

At a time when their own boundaries are so vague, adolescents feel secure if other boundaries just beyond them are well defined. There is a measure of security in sensible limits based on values they share with their parents.

In the next chapter we look at ways of identifying and combating drug use in adolescents. But prevention is better than cure, so we also look at how to create the kind of environment in which the growing child will not even be tempted to try drugs. Or, if tempted, knows to leave well alone.

WHAT CAN WE DO?

DON'T JUST SIT THERE, MAKE A LIST

One of the most painful things a parent can endure is seeing a once bright loving child fall hopelessly short of her or his full potential, or worse, seeing them lying full stretch on a mortuary table.

Society as a whole and parents in particular go to great lengths to protect children. We build fences around swimming pools so that toddlers won't fall in. We teach children to swim so that they won't drown. We insist that they wear safety helmets when riding bikes. We teach children about stranger danger, how to cross busy streets, how to combat bullying, how to look after themselves in the wilderness. We spend a fortune on education, health care, clothing, sport, music, arts and recreation, yet we spend hardly any money on, commit little time to and devote minimal effort to drug education.

Drug use and abuse is potentially the most destructive activity that children can become involved in. In many communities the majority of crimes, many of the road accidents, most of the workplace accidents and absenteeism, are drug-related.

And the age of experimentation with drugs is getting younger: eight-year-olds are now at risk in some communities. Drug distribution has become more sophisticated, drugs are now more readily available, they come in a wider variety and their potency has increased.

Here are some things that you as a parent can do to minimise the risks:
- ♦ Be constantly vigilant in regard to your child's attitude.
- ♦ Be aware of your child's social environment.
- ♦ Find the time to be around your child's activities.
- ♦ Find the time to be an active listener. Turn off the TV, the radio and the stereo. Put

> "Every time you pick up the tab for obnoxious behaviour, you have just paid for the next round."

down the book or newspaper and pay your child some attention.

♦ Be assertive and accommodating in your guidance.

♦ Be aware of where your child is at night and be awake when they come home.

♦ Get children involved in the family decision-making process.

♦ Tell them your concerns where appropriate. You are their role model, and if at times you feel inadequate, then share this with them and they will respond to your honesty and humanity.

♦ Encourage your child to play some sport; make sure he or she eats three healthy meals a day and gets plenty of regular sleep.

♦ Make sure your child feels needed, wanted and respected.

♦ Learn the telltale signs of substance abuse (see Chapter 2).

♦ When it becomes obvious that your child is in trouble, when the signs of substance abuse are irrefutable and you want to push the panic button, it's time to sit down and take a deep breath.

♦ Do not over react. Discuss the situation dispassionately with the whole family. Keep a constructive dialogue going with the child who's abusing drugs while you buy time to seek expert advice.

♦ Educate yourself on the real dangers of substance abuse. You will be in direct competition with some self-declared authorities in the playground and wider community. At this stage children and adolescents think they know more about drugs than you do, and

they are probably right. On the other hand, teenagers' drug education is given to them by drug dealers whose primary motivation is profit, or by users who get their supplies subsidised by new recruits.

♦ Remember your ultimate goal is to get your child off drugs. Half-measures will avail you of nothing. The child has to be told that abuse of drugs in any form is an abuse of the whole family. The whole family will bear the consequences of the lying, the stealing and the heart-break. Accordingly the whole family has a right to make some input.

♦ Parental discipline needs to be rational and sensible. Love has to be tough. Every time you pick up the tab for obnoxious behaviour, you have just paid for the next round.

♦ Contact the parents of friends of your child who might also be on drugs. Combined parent power is stronger than children's peer pressure groups. No-one - not even their best friends - loves your child as much as you do. If there is no parent group at your child's school, then start one with the help of the Parent Teachers Association.

♦ Work with and support principals, teachers, police youth aid initiatives and drug education programmes. Prevention can work when everyone works together. Most towns have a citizens advice bureau that can direct you to the experienced agencies in your area. Look them up in your telephone book. If dissatisfied with the help

"Your responsibility as a parent is not as great as you might imagine. You need not supply the world with the next conqueror of disease or major motion picture star. If your child simply grows up to be someone who does not use the word 'collectible' as a noun, you can consider yourself an unqualified success."

FRAN LEBOWITZ

they offer, you may need to widen your search.

♦ If your child has broken the law you will probably agonise over whether or not you should notify the police. Mind you, while you're wringing your hands, there is every chance the police will eventually be notifying you. In some communities, contacting the police would be a retrograde step. Where you have enlightened law enforcement agencies, police intervention can be enormously beneficial.

♦ Contact your doctor, and if he or she says marijuana is nothing to worry about, then it's time to start worrying about your doctor.

♦ Treat with caution the gospel of some social scientists who insist that a "safe" drug is merely a dangerous drug that a child or adolescent has not been taught how to use correctly. There is no such thing as children's safe use of addictive and harmful substances, just as there is no safe way to play Russian roulette.

♦ Avoid the "you need me" drug treatment agencies that push the line that the drug problem will never go away, therefore our children need to be taught how to use drugs properly. This is a popular philosophy in some quarters, because it is what all users want to hear. An addict told that he can stay on drugs forever as long as he learns how to manage his addiction is hardly likely to opt for the rigours of total abstinence.

Because there can be no cure under this approach, therapists from this school of thought run no risk of running out of clientele; indeed, they are more likely to develop long waiting lists made up of addicts who can hardly believe their luck.

STAYING DRUG-FREE

If and when you make a breakthrough with your child, and he or she accepts the importance of delaying all decisions on drugs until they are through maturation, there are a number of things you can do to help them clear the drugs from their system.

♦ Ensure they eat three nutritious meals a day. A dietitian can advise you here. Adolescents need a well-balanced diet rich in minerals and vitamins to provide the brain and body with the nutrients essential to normal development.

♦ Encourage them to exercise in a sport they enjoy, ensuring they get

up a sweat that will speed up the elimination of toxins from the body. Exercise increases the aerobic capacity of the adolescent, pushing essential oxygen to all areas of the body, stimulating growth, aiding digestion and facilitating the natural desire for a good night's sleep.

♦ Regular sleep is essential. Sleep is when the body's batteries are being recharged - when the next day's neurochemicals are being manufactured.

♦ Get them to drink lots of fluids to help flush the system. Short courses of vitamins, especially B and C, can be very beneficial.

♦ Get them to practice deep breathing in fresh air. This will help to improve oxygen levels in blood travelling to the brain.

♦ Give them love based on mutual respect. Tell them repeatedly that you love them and that it is only the bad drug-induced behaviour that you loathe.

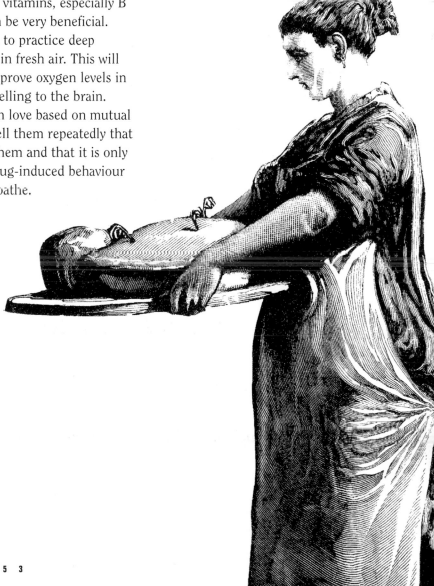

KIDS, THIS IS FOR YOU

20 WAYS TO SAY NO TO DRUGS

Giving advice to teenagers can be likened to attempting to slow a speeding locomotive with a horseshoe magnet. You know it's an almost hopeless cause, and it won't do your stress levels any good, but sometimes miracles can occur. Actually, most of what follows in this chapter isn't advice at all- it's what most adolescents know instinctively anyway.

Kids, this is for you:

- ♦ Look after your brain - it's the only one you've got.
- ♦ Be aware of your parents' concerns.
- ♦ Be aware of their efforts to provide for your needs, in not always easy circumstances.
- ♦ Be aware of your parents' interests and hobbies.
- ♦ Be accommodating of your parents' guidelines.
- ♦ Respect your parents' rules, boundaries and curfews.
- ♦ Be aware that one day you will probably be a struggling parent, baffled by teenagers of your own.
- ♦ Delay decisions about the use of legal and illegal substances until you have completed maturation.
- ♦ Remember that the most crucial stage of the secondary evolution of the brain is still being acted out right into your late teens and early 20s.
- ♦ Chemical vandalism of the maturation process drastically reduces the 10,000 potential connections that your 100 billion neurons are capable of making. The less connections you make, the less of the essential you there is. You have everything to lose and nothing to gain by becoming a diminished version of what you could have been.

> "Remember that as a teenager you are in the last stage of your life when you will be happy to hear that the phone is for you."
>
> - Fran Lebowitz

20 WAYS TO SAY NO TO DRUGS AT A PARTY WITHOUT FEELING LIKE A DWEEB

1. Not for me, thanks, I'm a dweeb.

2. No thanks, I'm driving.

3. I'd rather not - I was kind of hoping to use my brain to make a living.

4. Hey, I get high on life. Seriously though, I'm snorting toilet bowl cleaner at the moment, and I'd rather not mix my poisons - if you know what I mean.

5. No way. Last time I touched that stuff I went home, tidied my room, mowed the lawns and washed the car. It was really scary, man.

6. I'm on pretty heavy medication for schizophrenia, so I should decline. Funny - half of me wants to say yes and the other half wants to say "Hi there, earthlings, I come in peace..."

7. Drugs? What drugs? Where? Oh, I see, that stuff right there. Jeez, I think I might have had enough already.

8. Sorry, I never touch anything I haven't grown, mixed, distilled or stolen myself. It's a little hang-up of mine ever since I sucked on what I thought was a throat lozenge at a fourth-form party and woke up as a sex slave on a Russian trawler operating out of Vladivostok.

9. The last time I did this it turned out to be horse tranquillizer. I sprained my ankle on the way home and it took me hours to persuade a panel of vets that I shouldn't be put down.

10. Oh boy. I'm taking a risk here. My short-term memory is pretty shagged as it is... I'm sorry, what were you offering me again?

11. I don't smoke. If you want to make me hash cookies, or better still, pavlova, I'm a starter, but don't go to any trouble.

12. Have you got anything that won't make me projectile-vomit without warning?

13. I can't. I'm an undercover cop. I'll have one at home when I'm off-duty.

14. You wouldn't really want me sharing that. I've got these weeping boils on my gums that just won't heal.

15. I'll pass. I have enough trouble getting erections as it is.

16. No thanks, my I.Q. is dangerously low already.

17. Pills scare me. The lady next door took liver pills all her life and when she died they had to beat her liver to death with a pick handle.

18. My parole officer wouldn't approve. He says the next time I pull someone's head off when I'm stoned I won't get off with periodic detention.

19. Have you got anything stronger? I mean, really strong. I'm into ECT right now. Smelling your own hair burning is really something else, man.

20. Call me wild and crazy, but I'm strictly a hot-milk-and-cocoa guy.

In point of fact, if you don't want to take drugs you don't have to explain or justify your actions to anyone. A polite but firm refusal is your prerogative. Better still, simply passing a joint or tab on to the next person without saying a word is a pretty powerful statement in itself.

A SISTER'S STORY

A SIBLING SLAYS THE DRAGON

I knew things weren't right, but I didn't know exactly what was wrong. I didn't see my brother as much as I used to, and put it down to the fact he was just too busy.

Then one day a mutual friend sat me down and said, "Have you noticed anything about your brother lately?" What had I noticed? Nothing specific. He was more unreliable than he used to be, not that he was very dependable to begin with. He used to get on really well with my husband, children, and our Mum, but now he didn't seem to have the time nor the interest.

I had no answer to the question I had been asked. I had noticed lots of things and nothing. "He's using." That's all the friend said. In those moments everything changed. He may as well have said, "Your brother's going to die." To me it meant the same thing.

My older sister died of an overdose when she was 20. I was 18 then. Now my younger brother was going down the same track. How the hell could he do it? He loved her, he knew what happened, he even had a photo of her in his bedroom.

It is a curious thing, but I suspect the pain my brother felt in himself that led him to use drugs could not have been as great as the pain he then inflicted on himself as the using went on. Inevitably he also caused great agony to those around him.

All I could think about was how to save him. I figured the first thing I had to do was get him to admit what he was doing. I vainly hoped that if this was open between us he might stop, or when things got really bad he could come to me and I could look after him. I became obsessed with this idea and decided to confront him. I felt I only had one shot because if I failed then to get this thing in the open, he could shut me off forever, refuse to see me, refuse to talk to me.

So I asked him the question. "Are you using?" Of course not. "Then show me your arms." (I realised later it could have been wrists, ankles, all sorts of places.) He wouldn't. I threatened to tell Mum what I suspected if he didn't own up. I threatened to tell the whole extended

> "Layered over the person we knew and loved was the hard shell of lies and ruthlessness an addict needs to survive."

family. I threatened to tell the people he worked with. We argued round in a circle with lots of "how dare you say that/do that/think that," on both sides. Not only did I threaten him though, he threatened me, physically. I had cornered him and he was fighting. It was when he nearly hit me that I started to cry, and it was then he hugged me. For a moment I saw the brother I knew and loved.

If I had known what it would be like, I would never have confronted him in that way. It was a tortuous, anguished one hour hell that only those people you love a whole lot can ever put you through. But I brought that on myself. I was doing what I thought I needed to do, and so was he. Finally he said, "Yes, I'm using, but you didn't hear me say that." He promised to talk to me about it later and drove off. I knew he wouldn't talk later. His partner had been toughened up by using for years and she would never let him talk to me about it. Never admit it, that was the cardinal rule.

After that came two years of hell. I'd see him occasionally, always totally absorbed with himself and what he was doing. Family gatherings became a misery as with pinned eyes he and his partner fizzed and then fell into stupor.

Eventually money became in short supply. It was going up his arms at an extraordinary rate. He was also trying to get a business going and was constantly looking for investors. He would come to see me with his schemes involving fantastic potential returns and opportunities of a lifetime. They were so close to production, all I had to do was give him a few thousand dollars and the profits would pour in. The plea was the same over and over.

He had all the pieces of paper looking right, all the words right and he looked the part - a smart young businessman founding a manufacturing empire. Some pretty hardened bankers believed him too, but then they were missing a key piece of information. Creditors put caveats on family-owned property he had borrowed against without our knowledge, the debts climbed and the assets began to disappear.

As his life became increasingly desperate, everything that wasn't mortgaged was sold and everything that was mortgaged had reached the limit. He had borrowed as far as he could. Payback time was closing in on him.

One evening my mother phoned to say he had called, desperate and wanting to see her. He needed help. She was very concerned, but she couldn't take any more scenes with him. A moment later he phoned me, sounding very level but said he needed to see me that night, was 10 o'clock too late? I thought this is it, it's crunch time, he's hit bottom. Now he will come to me for help to get clean.

When he arrived he bore no resemblance to the son who had pleaded with his mother. He was back with another fantastic deal. It brought home to me the desperate game of manipulation he was playing. What was going to get the most money out of us? "I need money to feed your grandchildren", or "have I got a deal for you".

I cried that night thinking it was for him, but it was for me. He was never going to come to me for real help. He was not going to give me the chance to save him. And if he did die it was going to be alone, away from us who loved him most.

To cut off someone you love is an agonising thing but every time we supported him in the way he wanted we merely helped him perpetuate his addiction and the shared nightmare that went with it. Layered over the person we knew and loved was the hard shell of lies and ruthlessness an addict needs to survive. It was when we got glimpses of the real person we used to know hiding inside that it shattered us. The kind and generous person we used to know was killing himself and we couldn't save him. The addict we had come to know was a horrifying distortion with a clearly defined list of priorities. Drugs, money, drugs, money.

Through the hell years I ran a pretty constant harassment. I kept it in his face and he hated me. I was hurting him. It made no difference to what happened. Sometimes I wanted him to die, the grief was already so great. I got counselling which helped. I cultivated a stomach ulcer and heart trouble which didn't help. Now I wish I had loved him more and harassed and hurt him less during that time.

As he slid to the bottom, every time the phone rang I was expecting either abuse or a call that told me he was dead.

I don't know what day it was that he decided to change his life. He announced he was going into treatment and took himself to detox then on to a treatment centre. At first we suspected it was to lull us into writing cheques. Any trust we had in him had been shattered long before.

He was away for five months. I did not see him during that time though Mum did. Then one day he was back, and I arrived home to find him sitting on the deck waiting for me. That was three years ago.

Initially it was a tenuous time for all of us as wounds healed and we came to forgive and to know each other again. But soon I found it wasn't my old brother I got back, it was a new version, an improved version. The most caring and gifted soul emerged. He has a love and enthusiasm for people and life that is wonderful to be around. God, what a frightening and painful time, but it was the most miraculous experience, for all of us.

This is not his story, it is mine. His story is also about pain and anguish - it is just that we suffered from different sides. Now though, the joy is shared together.

- Anne

Footnote: *When I finished writing this I asked my brother to read it. It was a scary moment for both of us. Although we had come to understand each other we had never discussed specifics. We were both in tears at the end. I asked what had turned him round. He told me that one day he decided to listen to his heart.*

GETTING OFF DRUGS

ONLY YOU CAN CHOOSE

If you have been taking mind-altering substances for 12 months or more, there is every chance you will have been eating poorly during that period. Your diet will probably have been low in essential trace elements - in particular you will probably have an iron deficiency. Less iron means that your body makes fewer red blood cells, which in turn means that your blood carries less oxygen from the lungs to the rest of the body.

The burning of glucose gives cells their energy, but cells deprived of oxygen can't burn as much glucose as they would normally. Tired cells go about their housekeeping less efficiently. Nutrients are not pumped properly into cells - the groceries are not delivered - waste products are not pumped out - the rubbish is not collected.

To check this out and for other tests, you will need to see your doctor. Ideally your parents or caregivers should organise this and go with you. If you are on your own, or if your parents or caregivers are not interested or use drugs themselves, you will have to make the appointment yourself.

Once there, insist on a full medical examination with a toxicology test including drug screening, a trace element test and the liver function test.

These simple, painless tests can save not only lives but many hours of handwringing and analysis working out why someone is suddenly behaving strangely.

People who sniff solvents risk poisoning from lead, polymers and toxins that can trigger aggression and depression. Anaemia alone will make some teenagers nut off.

You should also get the doctor to check your immune system and check you for sexually transmitted diseases.

Kicking drugs on your own is not easy. Kicking drugs with an army of therapists lending you support is not easy either. Basically people get well when they, and they alone, elect to change their behaviour. But there are things you can do to help make that decision stick.

10 ACTIONS THAT WILL HELP YOU KICK DRUGS

1. Increase your fluid intake. Drink at least half a gallon of water or natural fruit juice a day. This helps to flush toxic substances out of your system. It will have you heading to the bathroom all hours of the day and night but wearing out the carpet is a lot better than chewing it.

2. You should take up some form of exercise that has you producing one good sweat a day. Regular exercise increases oxygenation of the blood, and sweating helps to flush toxins out of the body. Regular exercise will also help you to sleep better at night.

3. Learn some relaxation and deep-breathing exercises. Do them every morning and at night.

4. If you experience withdrawal symptoms, if you get a little sweaty and panicky, get into a warm shower and slowly lower the temperature. In most instances the anxiety will fade.

5. If you find withdrawal too much, then contact the younger members of support groups, such as

Narcotics Anonymous and Alcoholics Anonymous. At no cost and with absolute confidentiality they will provide the peer support and friendship desperately needed by those who are badly addicted.

6. Take a short course of vitamins B6 and B12. Alternate a capsule each day for six to eight weeks, then follow that with a four-week course of 500mg vitamin C. Drug abuse suppresses the immune system and this will give your body a gentle boost.

7. Eat sensibly. A nutritious diet is cheap and is essential to the brain's and the body's recovery. After exposure to toxins, a short session with someone who knows something about diet would be invaluable.

8. Go to bed at a sensible hour and get a good night's sleep in a well-ventilated room. Avoid coffee and alcohol for several hours before going to bed. It is during sleep that your brain manufactures all the chemicals it will need the next day.

Despite the fact that the rest of your body - apart from the heart and the lungs - is resting, during sleep your brain sometimes requires as much oxygen as if you were playing tennis. Don't take sleeping pills - parts of your brain have to be wide awake if the rest of your brain is to sleep properly.

9. Treat yourself to safe hobbies and interests that will develop your motivational skills and enhance your enjoyment of life - be it in music, art, sport or whatever else takes your fancy.

10. When you make it, don't be afraid to pass on your hard-won knowledge and experience to any friend who needs to undertake the same journey. There is bound to be resistance at first, but if it works out you will have made a true friend for life, and you will be that much stronger yourself.

A COUNSELLOR'S STORY

THE THREE-MONTH CHALLENGE

The first thing I noticed about Jacob was his size. He was the tallest of the surly boys waiting for me in the headmaster's office the afternoon I was called in to help. He came from a typical New Zealand family, academically he was average, but he possessed truly remarkable ability in one particular sport that he loved.

He had represented his school in this sport and taken provincial titles as he progressed through the age groups. His rapid improvement ended at the age of 16 when he started using drugs.

He was suspended from a large high school along with six other students for marijuana and other drug use. Their teachers had observed dramatic changes in behaviour and attitude. After police investigations I was called in to the school to assist. Two boys were ultimately expelled for possessing and distributing drugs. One is now dead as a result of a drug overdose; he was only 18.

All of the boys displayed diminished interest in schoolwork, arrogant and obnoxious attitudes toward parents and teachers and short-term memory loss. Jacob was ordered to counselling. He presented himself to me with a "Who gives a shit?" attitude. Indeed, when I spelt out the seriousness of the situation to him, those were his very words. His provincial sports coach had also thrown him out of the team. This devastated Jacob, as it was the one thing he still seemed to care about.

Initial blood tests confirmed the use of marijuana and an hallucinogenic substance. When confronted, Jacob opened up and told me the whole story of the group's secret experimentations with drugs - the direct result of one of them purchasing a book from a Head Shop (a shop specialising in literature advocating drug use).

Jacob was permitted to return to the school

> "The disciplines and rigours of top-level sport quickly sort out the dedicated from the medicated."

under strict conditions, which included counselling. It was a difficult and lonely time for him. He was missing his sport but his coach held his ground, insisting he would need to be clean for an extended period of time if he wanted reinstatement in the squad.

I struck up a strong bond with him. We agreed on a contract. I would help him with all his problems and in return, if after three months he remained drug-free, I would approach his coach about giving him another chance. He also had to show more respect for his parents and teachers, to submit voluntarily to random urinalysis tests and, whenever I said "Jump!", he had to reply "How high?"

Three months later, having kept his end of the bargain, Jacob was back in the provincial squad performing better than ever and setting his sights on a national title. The disciplines and rigours of top-level sport quickly sort out the dedicated from the medicated, and Jacob was starting to excel.

His training and travel costs began to mount. Coming from a decent family of modest means it became clear that cash would have to be found if he was going to fully realise his exceptional potential. I approached two businessmen for help. Impressed by the strength of character Jacob had shown in overcoming his drug problem, they generously provided the necessary sponsorship.

In 1994 all three of us were present and immensely proud when Jacob won two national titles. He has since represented New Zealand overseas and is now an Olympic medal prospect.

There are many heartbreaks and disappointments in counselling. Jacob was one of the success stories. To meet him when he was at a crossroads and to witness his recovery and the triumphant way he took control of his life again has been a truly gratifying experience.

- *Joseph*

"We agreed that if after three months he remained drug free I would approach his coach about giving him another chance."

CHAPTER 15

CONCLUSION

This book has only one purpose: to equip children and adolescents, their parents, guardians, teachers, community agencies and society at large with some simple facts about some very complicated substances.

What adults choose to sniff, snort, smoke, ingest or inject into their bodies is not our immediate concern. It has to be assumed that adults have some choice over their own behaviour. In theory anyway, they should be capable of understanding the legal, physiological, mental and emotional risks they are taking when they abuse drugs.

Children and adolescents need to know that you can't buy euphoria - at best you can lease it temporarily, but the premiums are high. Life has to be faced head-on, on life's terms. If you use a week's supply of the body's own feel-good chemicals in a single afternoon, you go into pharmaceutical debt to yourself. There is no denying emotional pain or hurt, but the sorrow you mask today is the sorrow you experience with interest tomorrow.

Life is hard, but as a blues singer once said, if it weren't for the rocks in its bed, the stream would have no music.

I do not wish you joy without a sorrow,
Nor endless days without the healing dark,
Nor brilliant sun without the restful shadow,
Nor tides that never turn against your barque.

I wish you faith and strength and wisdom and love,
Goods gold enough to help life's needy ones.
I wish you songs but also blessed silence
and God's sweet peace when every day is done.

A poem carved on the wall of an 18th century Baltimore church.

"I know that most men can seldom accept even the most obvious truth if it would oblige them to admit the falsity of conclusions which they proudly taught to others, and which they have woven, thread by thread, into the fabric of their lives."

Leo Tolstoy

THE DANGER LIST

FROM ALCOHOL TO STEROIDS:
A READY-REFERENCE GUIDE
TO ALL THE MAJOR DRUGS

Alcohol

First the man takes the drink, then the drink takes a drink, then the drink takes the man.
Japanese proverb

Most people who drink alcohol find it a useful social facilitator, a normal part of occasions happy and sad, and they have no problems with it. For those addicted to its use, however, alcohol is the occasion.

SOURCE:
The product of the fermentation of complex carbohydrates and sugars in fruits, vegetables and grains.

HISTORY:
The first instance of alcohol abuse is recorded in the book of Genesis. (After the Great Flood, Noah got drunk and disgraced himself.) Alcoholic beverages of varying strength have been consumed all over the world for thousands of years, except in Islamic countries, where religion forbids their consumption.

NEUROTRANSMITTERS DEPLETED:
Gamma amino butyric acid (GABA).

BRAIN SITES AFFECTED:
Cerebral cortex, cerebellum and brain stem - particularly the breathing centre.

INITIAL MOOD ALTERATION:
Mild euphoria, relaxation and sedation.

ACUTE SIDE EFFECTS:
Intoxication, diminished hearing, diminished sense of responsibility, hangover.

CHRONIC SIDE EFFECTS:
Addiction, cirrhosis of the liver, memory impairment, reasoning impairment, Korsakoff's syndrome, foetal alcohol syndrome.

International statistics indicate that eight percent of those who drink alcohol will develop problems with it, and that each one of those victims will affect at least six other people.

When one is intoxicated with alcohol it is immediately obvious to all those around you, even if you insist loudly that you are as sober as a judge. This denial is harder to maintain in the morning, when you are suffering from a pounding headache, bloodshot eyes, sweats, nausea, tremors, memory loss and dry horrors, and there is something that looks suspiciously like last night's supper glued to your jacket lapels. Unlike drugs such as marijuana and LSD, alcohol has the virtue of giving its user plenty of signals of the damage being done.

Numerous studies report that low - repeat, low - doses of alcohol increase blood flow, accelerate heart rate, step up the transmission of nerve impulses, and excite simple spinal and brain-stem reflexes. Performance of highly complex problem-solving tasks is improved, memory and concentration are sharpened, and creative thinking is enhanced.

Initially alcohol can make the world seem a better place. After a while, however, alcohol's sedative effects take over from the stimulation, the pleasurable effects are cancelled out, and the average drinker stops drinking. People who don't stop at that point have the capacity to make the world a far worse place.

The active ingredient is ethyl alcohol (ethanol), a clear colourless inflammable substance that can be made synthetically or produced naturally by fermentation of fruits, vegetables or grains.

An adult liver can metabolise up to 30mls of alcohol an hour. (A can of beer, a glass of wine or a regular nip of spirits could contain from 15mls to 30mls of alcohol.) Drinking at a greater rate than this accumulates ethanol in the bloodstream.

Children and adolescents absorb alcohol faster than adults, and their livers metabolise it less efficiently. By their own admission many teenagers do not drink socially - they drink to get high, drunk, rat-faced, wasted etc.

Alcohol has a low molecular weight. It is highly water-soluble but less fat-soluble. Once consumed, alcohol is distributed throughout body water. Having less muscle and more fatty tissue than males, females have less body water for alcohol to move into, so it remains in the bloodstream in higher concentrations than for a male of the same weight. A British Medical Association study showed that one jug of beer will raise a males blood alcohol level to 60mg/100ml but the female's to 135mg/100ml.

When taken orally it is rapidly absorbed into the bloodstream from the stomach and small intestine and travels directly to the liver, where much of it is broken down into acetaldehyde.

"Alcohol is a very necessary article. It enables Parliament to do things at 11 at night that no sane person would do at 11 in the morning."

GEORGE BERNARD SHAW

If you had six drinks in an hour, one drink would be converted into acetaldehyde in the liver while the other five would slosh around in the bloodstream as ethanol.

Acetaldehyde is a poison. It acts as a cellular irritant and, in high concentrations, causes damage, spilling into the bloodstream and travelling to the brain, where it interferes with brain amines acting as neuro-transmitters. The various symptoms of acetaldehyde poisoning are known collectively as a hangover.

Persistent acetaldehyde poisoning causes liver cells to perform poorly: some die and are replaced with fat and fibre. This is cirrhosis of the liver.

The latest studies show that over time ethanol reduces the metabolic activity of the brain. It directly depresses the neurons of the respiratory centre in the brain stem, reducing oxygen uptake and making breathing less efficient.

When blood oxygen levels are progressively lowered, the first stage is euphoria. Then come sedation, drowsiness, sleep, anaesthesia, coma and death. Fortunately for the drinker it is very difficult to drink while you are sleeping, and only the supremely dedicated make it to the coma stage.

In 1953, the Welsh poet Dylan Thomas, returning to his New York hotel room after a drinking binge, proudly informed his girlfriend that he had just downed 18 whiskies in a row. He then fell unconscious, lapsed into a coma and died. (Alcohol may not have been the only culprit: the day before, Thomas's doctor had given him two morphine injections for a medical condition.)

Because it diminishes people's sense of responsibility, makes them more reckless, and can heighten rage and despair, intoxication is potentially life-threatening - especially when coupled with testosterone, the hormone of male aggression. Alcohol can be deadly if the intoxicated one is behind the wheel of a motor vehicle, is in possession of a loaded weapon, or wants to go white-water rafting at night. But deaths from actual alcohol overdose are rare.

They are more common when alcohol is combined with other drugs, particularly marijuana. One of the side effects of marijuana use is suppression of the vomiting centre in the brain stem.

An inactivated vomiting centre permits a drinker to consume alcohol in volumes that would normally have them spewing their guts out. The extra alcohol remains in the system at toxic levels, plunging the drinker into a coma and possibly death.

All of us, regardless of race, colour, creed or gender, have a stern, humourless voice somewhere in the back of our skulls telling us to sit up straight, to face the front and to mind our own business. It warns against staring down the front of girls' dresses or dancing suggestively with boys. It reminds us that we have work or school in the morning and that we should go to bed early.

The beauty of alcohol is that it shuts that voice up halfway through the first glass. The curse of alcohol is that after the fifth glass the blessed silence is sometimes broken by another voice insisting that if we put our foot down we can beat the train to the level crossing.

Some extreme alcoholics would rather drink than eat, and over time they suffer from a vitamin B (thiamine) deficiency. Thiamine is crucial in the metabolism of glucose - the brain's main fuel - and prolonged vitamin B deficiency causes brain damage known as Korsakoff's syndrome. Victims suffer from apathy, confusion and profound memory impairment.

In the womb the still-developing foetal liver is short on enzymes, rendering the unborn child particularly susceptible to toxins. The placenta serves as the unborn baby's stomach and lungs. It has a vast surface area permitting molecules in the mother's blood easy access to the foetal bloodstream. Ethanol and acetaldehyde, which cross unimpeded, can't be broken down, are not excreted by the undeveloped kidneys, and are thus free to wreak havoc and destruction at will - a condition known as foetal alcohol syndrome. Ethanol moves freely through breast milk to the feeding baby.

DRUNK AT A PARTY: "Excuse me, do lemons have feathers?"

HOSTESS: "No."

DRUNK: "I'm dreadfully sorry, I seem to have just squeezed your canary into my gin."

Old Joke

ALCOHOL STREET SLANG NAMES.

BOOZE, JUICE, BREW, TURPS, PISS, PLONK, SAUCE, LUNATIC SOUP ETC.

DRINKING AND DRIVING

Alcohol consumption interferes with your ability to drive a motor vehicle safely.

♦ Alcohol slows down your reaction time by 10 to 30 percent - messages simply take longer to pass from your eyes to your brain; the processing of incoming information becomes harder, and instructions to your muscles don't travel as fast.

♦ Alcohol reduces your ability to do two or more tasks at time - drunks find it hard to drive and sing at the same time so they tend to, unfortunately, concentrate on the latter.

♦ Alcohol lowers your ability to see distant objects - night vision can be reduced by 25 percent and blurred, double vision and loss of peripheral vision can also occur.

♦ It's worth noting that successful Formula 1 racing drivers reach for bottles of champagne **AFTER** the race is won, and even then they spray most of it over each other rather than actually drink the stuff.

Alcohol helps create a false sense of security and overconfidence, with the result that intoxicated people are prepared to take greater risks. It is a fact that, even when perfectly sober, young drivers are more accident prone than older, more experienced drivers. Younger people also have a lower tolerance to alcohol and this sharply increases their risk of having an accident when intoxicated - their bodies simply can't handle it as well. This susceptibility to alcohol is demonstrated by the lower average blood alcohol levels of young drink-driving offenders compared with older offenders when tested after an accident. The same pattern is found in drivers who are killed. Young drivers can drink less than their elders and get into more strife.

THE LAW

Drinking has been around forever, driving automobiles barely a hundred years, so it follows that laws against drinking and driving are a relatively recent phenomenon. The United Kingdom passed their first laws against drinking and driving in 1925; the United States followed a year later. The later landmark United Kingdom *1967 Road Safety Act* prescribed the limit for legal driving as 80 milligrams of alcohol per 100 millilitres of blood. Many countries followed suit and adopted similar legislation. These days,

"I was hitchhiking home after a hard night's drinking and a hearse stopped to ask if I needed a ride. I said, "No thanks . . . I'm not going that far."

ANON.

HALF THE COUNTRY HAVE TRIED IT. SOME OF THEM MANY TIMES...

WHEN THAT MANY PEOPLE BREAK THE LAW IT BRINGS THE WHOLE JUDICIAL SYSTEM INTO DISREPUTE...

breathalysers and other devices that measure blood alcohol concentration are used by law enforcement agencies everywhere in the battle against drinking and driving.

> **"Have you ever noticed, anybody going slower than you is an idiot, and anyone going faster than you is a maniac."**
>
> **GEORGE CARLIN**

BISHOPS, NUNS OFF-DUTY COPS, SCHOOLTEACHERS, ALL SORTS OF PEOPLE DO IT. CLEARLY PROHIBITION HAS FAILED...

IT'S TIME TO LEGALISE EXCEEDING THE SPEED LIMIT...

The legal consequences of driving while under the influence of alcohol vary from country to country - from fines, loss of driver's license, confiscation of motor vehicle to imprisonment. In Saudi Arabia, where any alcohol consumption is illegal, you can look forward to 75 lashes to go with your hangover.

DID YOU KNOW?
(Some stats from the States)

♦ According to the National Highway Traffic Safety Administration an alcohol-related death occurs about every 30 minutes in the USA.

♦ In the US car accidents have killed more people than all the American war fatalities put together.

♦ Alcohol-related highway crashes are the main cause of death for young people in the United States.

♦ About 3 in every 10 Americans will be involved in an alcohol-related crash at some time in their lives.

♦ Most traffic accidents involving people aged between 16 and 24 occur between 8 o'clock at night and 8 o'clock in the morning - the most dangerous period being between midnight and 4 o'clock in the morning.

♦ For all crashes, the alcohol involvement rate was 5 percent during the week and 12 percent during the weekend.

♦ Saturday nights accounts for 21 percent of all teenage motor vehicle deaths.

♦ Each year, students spend US$5.5 billion on alcohol, more than they spend on soft drinks, tea, milk, juice, coffee or books combined.

HOW TO GET HOME SAFELY

♦ **Don't drink at all.** This is easier said than done, but for the single-minded this strategy is just about 100 percent effective if you are driving yourself home and if everyone else you meet on the road is also stone, cold sober.

♦ **Start with a non-alcoholic drink.** This will help you stay hydrated and also keep you aware of what you are drinking.

♦ **Eat and drink.** Eating food before or during drinking slows the rate at which alcohol is absorbed into the body - remember salty food will make you more thirsty, so stick with water.

♦ **Drink slowly.** Drinking slowly over time, rather than guzzling all at once, will moderate your intake.

♦ **Alternate each alcoholic drink with a non-alcoholic one.** Apart from slowing your drinking down, if you're dancing you will become dehydrated more quickly, so the non-alcoholic drink will help avoid this.

♦ **Drink no more than 6 standards drink if you are a male adult; 4 if female.** A standard drink of:
— beer is **300ml or one half pint**
— spirits is **25ml or one single measure**
— wine is **80ml or one small glass**

♦ **Think about how you're going to get home before you go out.** Arrange for a designated driver or for your parents or an older sibling to pick you up.

♦ **Don't put yourself in a vulnerable position by trying to walk home alone.** Make sure you have the taxi fare if you don't want to wake up your parents.

♦ **Stick with your mates.** If you can, try and make sure someone in your group isn't going to party too hard, so they can look after the others.

♦ **Look after your friends.** Don't let someone who is out of control go off alone.

♦ **Don't get into a car with someone who's been drinking.** Need we say more.

♦ **If it's safe to do so, arrange to sleep over at the party.**

♦ **Coffee, cold showers, vomiting and exercise will not sober you up.** These are definitely fallacies; only time allows your body to rid itself of alcohol.

HOW TO ID A DRUNKEN DRIVER

Police officers patrolling the road look out for the following:

♦ turning in a wide radius

♦ straddling a centre lane marker

♦ almost striking an object or vehicle

♦ weaving through traffic erratically

♦ driving on something other than a designated road, like a footpath

♦ swerving to avoid traffic

♦ driving more than 10 kph below speed limit

♦ stopping without cause in traffic lane

♦ following another car too closely

♦ drifting off road surface

♦ braking erratically

♦ driving into opposing or crossing traffic

♦ signalling inconsistent with driving actions

♦ slow response to traffic signals

♦ stopping inappropriately

♦ turning abruptly or illegally

♦ accelerating or decelerating rapidly

♦ driving with headlights off.

Speeding is not a classic symptom of drunken driving. As speeding requires quicker judgment and sharper reflexes it may in fact indicate sobriety.

> "One more drink and I'd be under the host."
>
> **DOROTHY PARKER**

HOW TO IDENTIFY INTOXICATION

Police officers investigating an accident or an incident, look for the following:

♦ flushed face

♦ red, watery, glassy or bloodshot eyes

♦ smell of alcohol on breath

♦ slurred speech

♦ fumbling with wallet trying to get licence

♦ failure to comprehend the officer's questions

♦ staggering when exiting vehicle

♦ swaying/instability on feet

♦ leaning on car for support

♦ combative, argumentative, jovial or other inappropriate attitude

♦ soiled, rumpled, disorderly clothing

♦ stumbling while walking

♦ disorientation as to time and place

♦ inability to follow directions.

HAVING A PARTY?

If you're having friends over for a party follow these simply guidelines to ensure everyone has a safe and happy time.

♦ Establish house rules and let everyone know what they are.

♦ Think carefully about who you are inviting.

♦ Decide whether to serve alcohol, what to serve, and how much.

♦ Serve plenty of substantial food like pizzas, bread, and sausage rolls, not just chips and peanuts.

♦ Have plenty of non-alcoholic drinks available.

♦ Make arrangements for people to get home or to sleep over.

♦ Plan ahead about how to handle gatecrashers or people who won't stick to the party rules.

> **"When I read about the evils of drinking, I gave up reading."**
>
> **HENNY YOUNGMAN**

> **"If your children spend most of their time in other people's houses you're lucky; if they all congregate at your house, you're blessed."**
>
> **MIGNON McLAUGHLIN**

Amphetamines

Speed Kills
Road Code

Amphetamines act on the brain and body in much the same way as the more toxic naturally occurring drug cocaine. As the latter was subjected to increasing restriction and eventual prohibition, its role as a stimulant was taken over by the amphetamines.

SOURCE:
Amphetamines are synthetic compounds with similar stimulant properties to cocaine - in the body, they mimic adrenalin, noradrenalin and dopamine - but without any anaesthetic action.

HISTORY:
They were first synthesised by Los Angeles chemist Gordon Alles in the 1930s and marketed under the trade name Benzedrine. Amphetamine was the active ingredient in inhalers used in asthma treatment.

NEUROTRANSMITTERS DEPLETED:
Adrenalin, noradrenalin, dopamine.

INITIAL MOOD ALTERATION:
Amphetamines are powerful stimulants. They elevate mood, prevent sleep, suppress appetite and stave off fatigue.

ACUTE SIDE EFFECTS:
High blood pressure, strokes and (after large doses or an injection) overwhelming euphoria followed by devastating depression, exhaustion and confusion.

CHRONIC SIDE EFFECTS:
Addiction, fatigue, paranoia, psychosis.

During the Second World War the armed forces of many countries provided their soldiers and pilots with amphetamines - "pep pills" - to combat fatigue, elevate mood and increase endurance. In Japan at the same time, amphetamines were widely distributed to civilians working in factories, and at the war's end Japanese drug companies unloaded their massive stockpiles onto the demoralised populace as the ideal way to "replenish the

spirit". By the late 1940s five percent of Japanese adults were dependent on amphetamines.

Elsewhere, particularly in America, "pep pills" started appearing on the black market. Soon they were being used by students to help with their study, truck drivers to stay awake on long hauls, and athletes to sharpen their performance.

In the 1950s American soldiers in Korea and Japan began mixing amphetamines with heroin to make "speedballs" that were taken intravenously.

In the 1960s amphetamines were prescribed by doctors for the treatment of depression, narcolepsy and obesity. Widespread abuse of "diet pills" by housewives led to the re-examination of amphetamine use. The more it was studied, the more its dangerous similarity to cocaine use became apparent. Apart from the treatment of narcolepsy - a rare condition whereby sufferers spontaneously fall asleep - over the past 10 years there has been a marked decrease in the prescription of amphetamines by the medical profession; and sports bodies worldwide have banned their use by athletes. But street demand and black-market distribution is still booming.

While amphetamine use elevates mood and increases alertness, it also reduces the body's natural stores of adrenalin, leading to fatigue, depression and paranoia, and increasing the risk of brain, heart and lung blood vessel rupture.

Little is known about amphetamine use and pregnancy. There is some evidence of a withdrawal syndrome occurring in babies born to women using amphetamines extensively.

AMPHETAMINES STREET SLANG NAMES.

"A", AMT, BAM, BEANS, BENNIES, MOLLIES, TICKLERS, BROWNIES, CARTWHEELS, CRANK, CRYSTAL, DEXIES, DIET PILLS, DOLLS, FOOTBALL, HEARTS, LID POPPERS, LIGHTNING, PEP PILLS, RIPPERS, SPEED, THRUSTERS, UPPERS, UPPIES, UPS, WAKE-UPS AND A HOST OF OTHERS.

Barbiturates

She keeps running to the shelter of her mother's little helper.
Rolling Stones

SOURCE:
Synthetic - i.e., made in the laboratory.

HISTORY:
Barbiturates first came into use in the early years of the 20th century. Benzodiazepines were first synthesised in the late 1950s and valium - the most famous barbiturate - entered the market in 1963.

NEUROTRANSMITTERS DEPLETED:
GABA.

BRAIN SITE AFFECTED:
Gaba receptors in cortex and brain stem.

INITIAL MOOD ALTERATION:
Relief of anxiety and panic, sedation, sleepiness.

ACUTE SIDE EFFECTS:
Death from massive overdose, especially when combined with alcohol.

CHRONIC SIDE EFFECTS:
Crippling emotional and physical dependence, severe addiction.

Many psychiatrists define anxiety as a fear response in the absence of appropriate stimuli. Anxiety states can vary from the mild and disquieting to the severe and disabling. Barbiturates and benzodiazepines were developed to help treat anxiety.

In 1864 the Belgian chemist Adolph van Baeyer synthesised a powerful sleep-inducing drug from malonylurea and named it barbituric acid in honour of a friend called Barbara, who presumably was not the most animated person he had ever met.

In 1884 the first barbiturate for medical use - barbitone - was manufactured in Germany; in 1903 it was released for general use under the trade name Veronal.

Initially barbiturates were used to induce sleep, replacing alcohol, bromides and opiates such as laudanum. Since then, thousands of barbituric acid derivatives have been synthesised. Most are highly and dangerously addictive. Until very recently, "barbs" were the most used and abused of all the prescription drugs. These drugs, sometimes called sedative hypnotics, act as depressants in the brain, producing a calming, sleep-inducing effect.

They slow down the activity of the nerve pathways that control the emotions, breathing, heart action and some other functions. They work by mimicking or exaggerating the actions of the brain's own calming mechanism - the gaba (gamma amino butyric acid) neurotransmitters.

Barbiturates are broken down in the liver and eliminated by the kidneys at varying speeds according to their type. The slow-acting ones - mainly phenobarbitone and barbitone - reach the brain through the bloodstream in one to two hours. Their effects last six to 24 hours, with a half-life of 48 hours for phenobarbitone and 24 for barbitone.

The intermediate and fast-acting barbiturates - mainly secobarbitone and pentobarbitone - take effect in 20 to 45 minutes. The quick ones are the commonly known sleeping pills whose effects last only five or six hours, with little or no after effects when not abused.

Barb abusers favoured this group because the effects are similar to alcohol - in speed of impact, intoxication produced and subsequent addiction. This group has been identified with many suicides. The ultra-fast-acting barbiturates - mainly thiopentone (sodium pentothal) produce unconsciousness in a

BARBITURATES/ANXIOLYTICS HYPNOTICS STREET SLANG NAMES

BARBS, BEANS, BLACK BEAUTIES, BLOCKBUSTERS, BLUE ANGELS, BRAIN TICKLERS, DOWNERS, DOWNS, GOOFBALLS, GOOFERS, GREEN DRAGONS, MOTHER'S LITTLE HELPERS, NEMBIES, NIMBIES, PHENNIES, PINK LADIES, PURPLE HEARTS, SLEEPERS, YELLOW BULLETS, YELLOW JACKETS AND MANY OTHER MIND-BLOWING NAMES.

matter of seconds, which explains why their main use is for anaesthesia in hospitals. Sodium pentothal is also used as a truth serum by American police and for veterinary use when putting a cat or dog down.

The effects of barbiturate abuse during pregnancy are similar to those of alcohol. The drug is carried in the bloodstream, through the placenta, to the foetus. After the birth the baby will suffer from the usual symptoms of barbiturate withdrawal and impaired development due to brain damage in the womb.

Psychological dependence on barbiturates can develop very quickly. Physical dependence takes longer but is far more dangerous. It occurs when the body has grown so used to the presence of the drug that it reacts violently if the drug is suddenly withdrawn. Physical dependence to barbiturates and other sedative hypnotic drugs is one of the most deadly of all drug dependencies.

The withdrawal symptoms are worse than those of morphine or heroin. Death occurs in about five percent of those attempting withdrawal without supervised treatment, and some withdrawal effects can last for months - yet despite the rigours and risks